World War Two
A Very Peculiar History™

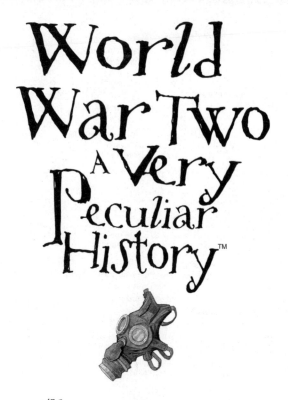

'You can no more win a war
than you can win an earthquake.'

Jeanette Rankin,
first female representative in the US Congress

World War Two

A Very Peculiar History™

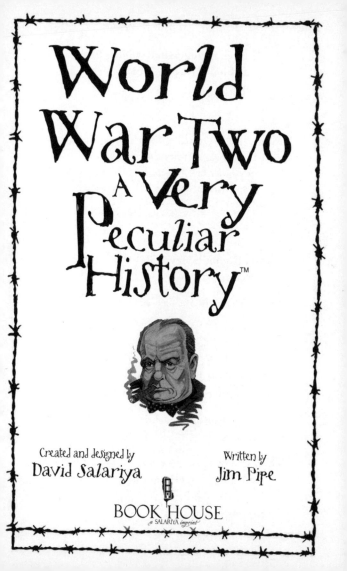

Created and designed by
David Salariya

Written by
Jim Pipe

BOOK HOUSE
a SALARIYA imprint

'I have never promised anything
but blood, tears, toil and sweat.'

Winston Churchill

'I swear that I would rather die in battle with
the enemy than surrender myself, my people
and my country to the Fascist invaders.
Blood for blood! Death for death!'

Russian war oath

'Goddam it, you'll never get the Purple Heart
hiding in a foxhole! Follow me!'

US Col. Henry P. 'Jim' Crowe, Guadalcanal, 1943

'And when he gets to Heaven
To St Peter he will tell:
"One more Marine reporting, Sir –
I've served my time in Hell."'

Sgt James A. Donahue, US Marine

'When this war is over I shall confine myself
entirely to writing and painting.'

Winston Churchill

Contents

❛We shall fight on the
beaches, we shall fight
on the landing grounds,
we shall fight in the fields
and in the streets,
we shall fight in the hills;
we shall never surrender.❜

Winston Churchill

INTRODUCTION

Heroes and villains

When I was growing up in the 1960s and 70s, just about every other film on TV seemed to be about World War Two. The conflict comes across as an adventure – dramatic, colourful and jam-packed with material tailor-made for the movies. Need heroes? Then there's John Wayne landing at D-Day in *The Longest Day* or Audie Murphy battling his way through Italy in *To Hell and Back*. Want humour? Watch as Clint Eastwood and his band of misfits sneak through the German lines to get their hands

on a secret stash of Nazi treasure in *Kelly's Heroes*. Meanwhile the Nazis make perfect movie villains. Telling the good guys from the bad guys couldn't be easier.

The films are very entertaining, but fact and fiction are often hard to tell apart. The real-life warriors depicted in *The Dambusters*, *The Great Escape* and *The Battle of Britain* aren't so different from the make-believe heroes in *The Guns of Navarone* or *Where Eagles Dare*. And when the shooting starts, the victims usually die cleanly and quickly.

More recent movies such as *Saving Private Ryan* don't pull any punches when it comes to showing the carnage on the battlefield. They acknowledge the horror, the heartbreak and the humanity of combatants on both sides. But the focus is still on the hardship and personal heroism of the soldiers.

Ten heroic war movies

1. **To Hell and Back** (1955). Audie Murphy was initially reluctant to star in this portrayal of his own real-life heroics in France and Italy, which won him the US Medal of Honor. Climbing onto a burning tank (which was on the verge of blowing up), he used its machine gun to stop a German attack almost single-handedly. Unlike most Hollywood pictures of the time – and at Murphy's insistance – his comrades are killed or wounded on screen as they were in real life.

2. **The Bridge on the River Kwai** (1957). This film focuses on the clash of wills between two military leaders. One is a Japanese prisoner-of-war (POW) camp commander, the other a British colonel determined to show British superiority by building the best possible bridge. Though based on a novel, the story was inspired by the building of a railway through Burma by British POWs in 1942–3.

3. **Ice Cold in Alex** (1958). Based on fact, this stars John Mills as a British army captain leading a plucky crew of misfits (including a German spy) across the desert back to British lines for a well-deserved pint. It took several takes to get the final scene right, by which time Mills was allegedly a little the worse for wear.

4. **The Guns of Navarone** (1961). This big-budget movie depicts the fictional destruction by British commandos and Greek partisans of two huge German guns during the Battle of Crete. It stars David Niven, who during the war served with the Commandos and took part in the D-Day landings.

5. **The Longest Day** (1962). This three-hour blockbuster, which tells the story of the D-Day landings on the coast of Normandy in June 1944, is packed with stars including John Wayne, Robert Mitchum, Richard Burton and Sean Connery. While clearing a section of the Normandy beach, the film crew uncovered a tank that had been buried in the sand since the original invasion.

6. **The Great Escape** (1963). Though the film is based on the true story of 76 Allied POWs who escaped from a German prison camp, the scriptwriters added a few thrills and spills of their own, including a memorable stunt where Steve McQueen's character leaps over a barbed-wire fence on a hijacked motorbike. In the film, several of the main heroes are American. In reality, almost all the escapees were British.

7. **Where Eagles Dare** (1968). Richard Burton and Clint Eastwood star as Allied secret agents who stage a daring raid on a castle where the Nazis are holding a US general prisoner. Not a film that stands up

to much scrutiny, historical or otherwise, with German soldiers falling like ninepins and a brown suitcase containing a limitless supply of dynamite, but it does include some spectacular moments, such as a dramatic cowboy-style fist fight on top of a cable car.

8. **Battle of Britain** (1969). Forget CGI: this retelling of the 1940 Battle of Britain used the real thing, including 12 Spitfires, 17 Me-109 fighters, 32 Heinkel bombers and a mountain of (blank) ammunition. The film is generally faithful to events, though many of the characters are only loosely based on real people.

9. **Schindler's List** (1993). Based on Thomas Keneally's largely factual novel *Schindler's Ark*, this film depicts the true story of a German businessman who employed Polish Jews as cheap labour in his factories and ended up saving 600 of them from being killed in the Auschwitz extermination camp. Though criticised for focusing on the survivors rather than the 6 million Jews who died in the Holocaust, it is a very moving film that gives a feeling of what it was like to be in a concentration camp.

10. **Saving Private Ryan** (1998). The film starts with a brutal depiction of the landing at Omaha Beach on D-Day. The movie was loosely based on a real story, in which a team is sent to rescue a US paratrooper whose three brothers have recently died in combat.

The courage of those on the front line and on the home front stirs the blood with good reason. Most combatants were ordinary people who did what they had to do in horrific circumstances. Even more incredible perhaps is the fact that so many put the trauma behind them and got on with their everyday lives after the war was over.

There is a danger, however, that action films are replacing real memories about the war. If you believe the movies, it was mostly won by the Americans with a bit of help from the British. By and large the film industry ignores the millions of Russians who died on the Eastern Front, the millions of troops from the British Empire who answered the call to arms, or the countless resistance fighters across Europe who risked not only their own lives but often those of their entire community.

Too rarely on screen do we see the true scale and savagery of the war, especially its impact on civilians. World War Two remains the largest single event in human history, fought across six of the world's seven continents and all of its oceans. Each of the four main

campaigns – in Russia, North Africa and the Mediterranean, Western Europe, and the Far East – was a major war in its own right.

It was also the most destructive conflict in history. It killed 70 million people, left hundreds of millions of others wounded in mind or body, cost more money and damaged more property than any other war in history. Thanks to the indiscriminate bombing of cities and the mass murder of civilians, everyone was in the front line. Until 1941, a British soldier was more likely to get a telegram to say that his wife had been killed in an air raid than the other way around.

Every twist and turn of the war brought a new nightmare: from the screaming dive bombers of the Blitzkrieg and the blistering heat of the North African desert to an icy death on the Russian front or the grisly fate of Japanese soldiers eaten alive by crocodiles on Pacific islands. The bloodbath only ended when the awesome power of the two first atomic bombs showed that doomsday was now only a skip and a jump away.

Daring raids, great escapes

There was no shortage of real heroism and daring escapes during the war:

British
- **Dambusters raid.** Using a 'bouncing bomb' specially developed by Barnes Wallis, the RAF's 617 Squadron of Lancaster bombers breached the Möhne and Edersee dams, flooding part of the Ruhr valley where much of Germany's heavy industry lay. The daring attack was a propaganda victory more than anything, and losses among the aircrew were high: 53 out of 133 were killed.

- **Operation Frankton.** Led by Major Herbert George Hasler, ten 'cockleshell heroes' paddled their canoes some 60 km to destroy German warships at Bordeaux. Six ships were damaged using limpet mines, but only two men survived the raid.

- **Operation Jaywick.** In September 1943, 14 commandos and sailors from the Z Special Unit sank seven Japanese ships in Singapore Harbour using limpet mines.

German
- **Operation Eiche (Oak).** On 12 September 1943, SS Captain Otto Skorzeny led a daring assault on the Gran Sasso Hotel in the Abruzzi mountains, where Italian dictator Mussolini was being held prisoner. The hotel

was taken in just four minutes with very few shots being fired. The getaway plane was overloaded and almost plunged into the valley floor before the pilot regained control. Mussolini was then flown to Hitler's HQ.

- **Sinking of the *Royal Oak*.** On 14 October 1939, U-boat ace Günther Prien volunteered to lead a daring raid into the anchorage of the Royal Navy's major base at Scapa Flow in Scotland. His submarine, *U-47*, sank the battleship HMS *Royal Oak* at anchor.

- **Escape from Camp 198.** On 10 March 1945, 67 German POWs tunnelled out of Camp 198 near Bridgend in South Wales and escaped over the sand dunes. Several POWs who stole a car were given a jump-start by British soldiers; then, pretending to be Norwegians, they picked up a hitchhiker who showed them the way to Gloucester. With one exception, all were eventually rounded up.

Norway
- **Operation Gunnerside.** On 16 February 1943, six Norwegian commandos were dropped by parachute from a British plane. Entering the heavily guarded Vemork power station in Telemark, Norway, via a cable tunnel, they used explosives to blow up the plant, and with it Germany's entire supply of heavy water, vital to is nuclear weapons programme. Despite having 3,000 German soldiers on their tail, all six escaped, five of them skiing 400 kilometres to Sweden.

American

- **The Doolittle Raid.** Led by Lieutenant-Colonel Jimmy Doolittle, this was the first raid by US bombers on Japan, on 18 April 1942. The raid boosted US morale after the Japanese attack on Pearl Harbor, but led to savage reprisals against the Chinese, who helped the US pilots after they were shot down.

- **Raid at Cabanatuan (Philippines).** On 30 January 1945, US Army Rangers, Alamo Scouts and Filipino guerrillas freed more than 500 POWs from a Japanese camp. After marching 48 km behind enemy lines to reach the camp, they surprised and killed some 700 Japanese soldiers.

Serbian

- **Operation Halyard.** Serbian Chetniks (guerrillas), led by General Draža Mihailović, rescued 512 allied airmen shot down over Nazi-occupied Serbia. It was the largest Allied airlift behind enemy lines during the war.

Japanese

- **Cowra breakout.** On 5 August 1944, over 540 Japanese POWs attempted to escape from a camp near Cowra in New South Wales, Australia. They flung themselves across the wire with the help of blankets. Armed with knives, baseball bats and clubs, they then stormed the machine-gun posts. Nearly half died in the attempt, and those that got away were soon rounded up; many committed suicide to avoid recapture.

Over 28 million people died in Russia alone. Though the Eastern Front rarely appears on the big screen, this is where much of the real slaughter of the war took place. The statistics tell a chilling story:

- **Out of every five German soldiers who died in the war, four died on the Eastern Front.**

- **Eighty per cent of Soviet men born in 1923 didn't survive the war.**

- **More Russians (military and civilians) lost their lives in the Siege of Leningrad than the total number of US and British soldiers who died in the whole war.**

Often forgotten is the fact that at least 20 million people died from starvation and resulting diseases during World War Two. During the Bengal famine of 1943, which killed three million Indians, one British journalist wrote that hunger 'is very dull' compared to the slaughter in combat.

Soldiers' talk

The military love of acronyms such as AWOL (Absent WithOut Leave) encouraged American soldiers to think up a few of their own to describe the chaos of the war.

- **FUBAR:** Fouled Up Beyond All Recognition
- **FUMTU:** Fouled Up More Than Usual
- **JANFU:** Joint Army–Navy Foul-Up
- **SNAFU:** Situation Normal: All Fouled Up
- **TARFU:** Things Are Really Fouled Up.

Acronyms were also used to send messages between servicemen and their sweethearts back home. They were usually written on the back of the envelope:

- **SWALK:** Sealed With A Loving Kiss
- **HOLLAND:** Hope Our Love Lives/Lasts And Never Dies
- **ITALY:** I Trust And Love You *or* I'm Thinking About Loving You
- **FRANCE:** Friendship Remains And Never Can End
- **BURMA:** Be Upstairs Ready, My Angel
- **MALAYA:** My Ardent Lips Await Your Arrival
- **BOLTOP:** Better On Lips Than On Paper.

For members of the armed forces, mail was second in importance only to food. In 1945, 2,533,938,330 pieces of mail were dispatched to the US Army.

Many British people suffered terribly during the Blitz, but by the end of the war they knew they were on the winning side, and they still had a homeland. Imagine what it was like for the Poles, many of whom lost everything, including family and home. Apart from the torture and slaughter of six million of their countrymen, much of their territory was annexed by Stalin's Soviet Union when the war ended, and those who returned risked death or arrest.

The horrors of war live on in the mind. My father still shudders when a local nightclub shines a bright light into the sky – he was 7 when the war began in 1939, and the searchlight is a painful reminder. Like many who lived through the war, he has never really talked about the details. Many servicemen returning home remained tight-lipped about what they had seen and done. My great-uncle served as a spy in North Africa, but no-one knew until years after his death when letters detailing his exploits came to light.

The British actor David Niven, a Normandy veteran himself, summed up how many felt:

'I was asked by some American friends to search out the grave of their son near Bastogne [in France]. I found it where they told me I would, but it was among 27,000 others, and I told myself that here, Niven, were 27,000 reasons why you should keep your mouth shut after the war.'

Many servicemen and civilians felt guilty that they had survived while so many others perished.

All too often, real memories of the war have been ignored in favour of national myths. In Britain, the glory of beating the Nazis has become part of the national identity. Before the World Cup final in 1966, reporter Vincent Mulchrone of the *Daily Mail* echoed the feelings of many when he wrote: 'Germany may beat us at our national sport today, but that would be only fair. We beat them twice at theirs.' Two generations after the war, England football fans still proudly wear T-shirts with the slogan 'Two World Wars and One World Cup'.

There has been some soul-searching over the savage bombing of Dresden by British and US forces, which destroyed the historic city

and killed tens of thousands of civilians. But many other shameful incidents, such as the Bengal famine, have been overlooked. At the same time, heroes who didn't fit the stereotype have been largely forgotten, such as the Indian Army soldiers, many of them Muslims, who won 38 Victoria Crosses and George Crosses – Britain's highest awards for valour.

It's no surprise that many countries chose to forget the real war. All in all, it was a bloody, shocking mess. Everything about it was extreme. Few leaders have been as tyrannical or paranoid as Hitler and Stalin. For pure evil, it is hard to match the Holocaust, the systematic murder of 12 million Jews, gypsies and others. Few warriors have ever been more fanatical than the Japanese kamikaze pilots who flew their planes into US warships.

Add to that incompetent generals, hare-brained schemes, treachery and betrayal, and it can be very hard to make sense of it all. Nothing – especially war – is ever simple. This little book can only scratch the surface – but hopefully it can give you some sense of just how mad it all was.

Skeletons in the closet

Almost every country involved in World War Two tells its own story about what happened:

- **Germany.** More than most, the Germans have faced up to what they did in the war. Students continue to take field trips to concentration camps, and in the last ten years several new memorials have been dedicated to the victims of the Holocaust.

- **France.** Under the Nazi-backed Vichy regime, French civil servants and police officers put over 75,000 Jews and other 'enemies of the state' onto trains bound for concentration camps. Yet until the mid-1990s, few ever talked about France's role in the Holocaust.

- **Italy.** Many Italian historians and politicians after the war focused on the struggle of the partisans and their help for the Allies, rather than on the atrocities committed by thousands of Italians under Mussolini and the Fascists.

- For decades, the **Austrians** called themselves the 'first victims of Nazism', glossing over the two million Austrians who cheered wildly for Hitler on his return to Vienna. Not a single Nazi war criminal has been put on trial in Austria in the last 40 years.

- Only recently has **Switzerland** taken a hard look at its role during the war, when Swiss banks traded looted Nazi gold for Swiss francs, effectively funding the Nazi war machine. Swiss ministers and generals gave orders to turn back 30,000 Jewish refugees at the Swiss border, knowing full well what would happen to them back in Germany.

- **Croatia.** Some 700,000 victims were murdered by Ante Pavelić's fascists, the Ustaše, during the war. The massacre was so horrific that the top German officers in Croatia, including SS commander Artur Phleps, urged Berlin to put a stop to it. Today, the victims and their surviving family members still await justice, while crowds at Croatian soccer games flaunt Ustaše and Nazi symbols and sing old fascist chants and songs.

- **Japan.** Japanese atrocities during the war were largely forgotten in the West, but not by POWs or by the Asian nations where they were committed. From 1941 to 1945, some 24 million people died in Japanese-occupied Asia. When the war ended, the Japanese immediately tried to rewrite history, and continue to do so.

- **Russia.** Russia still has problems facing up to the horrors of its own past, such as the mass rape of German women by the Red Army. Until recently, the story of what Russians call the 'Great Patriotic War' never dealt with the pact between Hitler and Stalin or the mass slaughter of the Poles.

> 6 I saw my enemies
> in Munich,
> and they are worms. 9

Adolf Hitler

CHAPTER ONE

THE ROAD TO WAR

I t's fairly easy to pin down the beginning of World War One. Following the assassination of the Austrian heir to the throne, Archduke Franz Ferdinand, the great European powers went to war during July 1914 like a line of falling dominoes. By August, battles were raging across the continent. Over the next four years, Italy, the United States and other nations around the world were dragged into the conflict.

But when did World War Two begin? Most Europeans would choose 1 September 1939,

when Germany invaded Poland. But you would probably get a very different answer from the Ethiopians gassed by the Italian air force in 1935, the people of Guernica in Spain who were bombed by German planes in 1937, or the Chinese whose relatives were among 300,000 massacred by Japanese forces in Nanking later that year.

In fact, it's been said that World War Two was really lots of little wars that turned into one stonking big one. It only went global on 7 December 1941, when the Japanese attack on Pearl Harbor prompted Hitler to declare war on the United States, having already conquered much of Europe.

Many historians wind back the clock even further, arguing that World War Two was a tragic but inevitable result of World War One, which ended on 11 November 1918. The 'Great War', as it was known at the time, had resulted in the death of millions of young men – 947,000 of them from the British Empire – while countless others returned home with terrible injuries.

Before you, de Gaulle

Shortly after the liberation of France in autumn 1944, General Charles de Gaulle, leader of the Free French forces, was inspecting a group of Resistance fighters in Toulouse. Pausing before one scruffily dressed man, he asked, 'And when did you join the Resistance?' The man replied 'Well before you, General'. He had fought against Fascist forces since the Spanish Civil War in 1936.

The three victorious leaders who put together the peace settlement – French premier Georges Clemenceau, British prime minister David Lloyd George and US president Woodrow Wilson – set out with the best intentions. By forcing harsh terms on the defeated Central Powers, they hoped to avoid a repeat of the war. The resulting Treaty of Versailles forced Germany to slash the size of its army and navy and to hand over its overseas colonies, while chunks of Germany were given to Belgium, Poland, France and Denmark.

The Treaty, however, went a step too far in blaming the Germans for the start of the war and demanding reparations (fines) of £6,600,000,000 for all the 'loss and damage' suffered by the Allies during the war. This led to a wave of anger in Germany, particular among German soldiers, who felt they had been 'stabbed in the back' by politicians. By the early 1930s this anger had turned into widespread support for the aggressive policies of Adolf Hitler, who had been a corporal during World War One.

The Allied leaders at Versailles also wanted to help smaller peoples to form their own nations. It was a noble idea, but Germany was now surrounded by a patchwork of weaker countries such as Poland and Czechoslovakia, who each owned bits of the old Germany. To a man like Hitler, this was a red rag to a bull.

Rise of the dictators

In the years after the Great War, most European countries were crippled by massive debts. Their economies struggled to recover, and the resulting hardship of the 1920s and 1930s led to extreme politics in many countries – most notably the National Socialist Party, or Nazis, in Germany, and the Fascists in Italy.

Right-wing groups could be found across Europe. In France, the Far Right leagues were a motley crew with a penchant for military parades and street brawls. Even so, the riots they orchestrated in February 1934 were enough to bring down the government. In Britain, the Conservative MP Sir Oswald Mosley was so taken with the Italian dictator Mussolini that he set up his own British Union of Fascists in 1932; they claimed to have 50,000 members at one point, and supporters included Lord Rothermere, the owner of the *Daily Mail* newspaper. Ireland had its own brand of Fascism in the 'Blueshirts', led by Eoin O'Duffy, the former head of police. O'Duffy organised marches, flags and salutes

based on those in Nazi Germany, though 'Hail O'Duffy' didn't quite have the same ring as 'Heil Hitler'.

In all these countries there was a desire for strong leadership and order. The first 'strongman' to make his mark was Italy's Benito Mussolini, known as *Il Duce* ('The Leader'). The son of a blacksmith, he rose to power in the 1920s, at a time when Italy was racked by strikes and street fighting. Mussolini swept to power in October 1922, promising to restore Italian pride. Anyone who stood in his way was ruthlessly murdered, and on Christmas Eve 1925 a new law effectively made him dictator. And when things started to go pear-shaped at home, Mussolini stirred up trouble abroad, promising to create a new Roman Empire.

In Germany, the bankrupt government simply printed money to solve its economic problems. This led to financial meltdown – cartoons of the time show people with wheelbarrows full of money unable to buy a loaf of bread. Like Mussolini, Adolf Hitler offered strong leadership. A cunning politician and a brilliant

speaker who could hold an audience spellbound, he was also a driven, unstable man. These qualities kept him going when other people might have given up, and persuaded others to believe in his vision – which was about to steer the world into an abyss.

In 1933 Hitler became Chancellor of Germany and swiftly made himself *Führer* ('Leader'). Posters, leaflets, radio and film, rallies and torchlit parades were all used to woo the German people in a propaganda onslaught organised by Joseph Goebbels, master of the 'Big Lie'. To attract young people to the party – and prepare them for war from a young age – he set up the Hitler Youth and the League of German Maidens.

'The English follow the principle that when one lies, one should lie big, and stick to it. They keep up their lies, even at the risk of looking ridiculous.'

Joseph Goebbels, 1941

Nazism in a nutshell

Hitler outlined his ideas in his book *Mein Kampf* ('My Struggle'), written in prison in 1923. During Hitler's years in power, the book was given free to every newlywed couple and every soldier fighting at the front. By 1945 it had sold over 10 million copies, making Hitler a millionaire.

The main ideas expressed in the book can be summarised very briefly as follows:

- **National Socialism.** In short: strong government, state control of the economy and complete obedience to the Führer.

- **A strong Germany.** All German-speaking people were to be united in one glorious country, which should become a world power.

- *Lebensraum.* This German nation needed 'living space' in which to expand. This would entail wiping out the Slav peoples in Eastern Europe and Russia and taking their lands.

- **The master race.** The Aryan race was superior to all other races, especially the Jews. ('Aryan' was a pseudo-scientific term which originally referred to speakers of the Indo-European family of languages; the Nazis used it to refer to those they regarded as pure-blooded Germans.)

- **Culture of hate.** Short on cash or fed up with your job? Nazis took out their frustration on Jews, communists, liberals, gypsies, gays and Jehovah's Witnesses.

- **Love of war.** Only in war, said Hitler, do humans show their true abilities – and only the strong survive.

Unfortunately, many Germans agreed with these poisonous ideas, and money earned from the book allowed Hitler to buy a Mercedes while still in prison. Hitler often supported his ideas with outright lies: he spread the myth that Jews had been responsible for Germany's defeat in World War One. Several Nazi ministers even resorted to mystical mumbo-jumbo to back up theories of the Aryan master race:

- **Heinrich Himmler**, head of the elite SS (*Schutz-Staffel* or 'protection squad'), believed his men were a new breed of supermen descended from King Arthur and his Knights of the Round Table. Himmler even organised an expedition in 1938 to find the secrets of the lost super-race in the mountains of Tibet.

- **Reichsminister Alfred Rosenberg** tried to prove that the Aryan race began on the legendary lost island of Atlantis. His book *The Myth of the Twentieth Century* was another Nazi bestseller, but even Hitler called it 'stuff nobody can understand'.

Hitler solved Germany's unemployment problem with a series of giant public works schemes. Then it was time to put into action his plan for a new world order based on Aryan 'racial purity'. The first step was to re-arm Germany and make her invincible. Anyone who disagreed was rounded up and put in a labour camp. Within six years, Germany was once again the most powerful country in Europe.

Another strongman appeared in Russia, where three years of civil war ravaged a country already on its knees at the end of the First World War. Millions died from famine, and the victorious Communists executed millions more or sent them to prison camps in Siberia. When Lenin, leader of the revolution, died in 1924, the power struggle to replace him was won by the wily Iosif Vissarionovich Djugashvili, better known to the world by his adopted name Stalin – 'Man of Steel'.

Stalin pushed through enormous economic changes, known as the Five-Year Plans. These catapulted Russia from an agrarian country into a major industrial nation, but at an

appalling cost. Millions of peasants were forced to give up their land and work on large, government-run farms. Many opposed the change and died in brutal crackdowns. On big engineering projects such as dams or canals, political opponents or Jews were used as slave labour. The Russian dictator's 'purges' of the late 1930s led to millions of people, including many army officers, being imprisoned in camps or executed.

'We are fifty or a hundred years behind the advanced countries. We must make good the difference in 10 years or they will crush us'.

Stalin, already suspicious of Germany, in 1931

Japan had its own economic woes. From the early 1930s onwards, the Japanese military got more and more involved in politics. When several politicians were assassinated in 1936, the terrified government agreed to hand over power. Though there was no single dictator, the generals had a similar control over the Japanese population. And, like Hitler and Mussolini, their ambition was to boost their country's economy by building a new empire – in their case, across the whole Pacific.

Peacemongers

Why didn't anyone stand up to these bullies?
The European victors of 1918, France and
Britain, had struggled to get their economies
back on track in the 1920s. America fared
better, but the collapse of the Stock Market on
29 October 1929 (known as Black Tuesday)
led to mass unemployment and poverty across
the globe. This Great Depression, as it was
called, would only end when American
factories began churning out weapons and
equipment in 1941.

Most people simply did not want to get
involved in another war. As late as 1940,
President Roosevelt promised to young
recruits: 'You boys are not going to be sent
into any foreign war' – though he privately
admitted that war was inevitable. In Britain
and France, many people joined campaigns
for peace in the 1930s. The few lone voices
who argued for tougher action, such as
Winston Churchill, were distinctly unpopular.
So, while Japan and Germany rearmed as
quickly as they could, most other nations were
reducing their fighting forces.

Nicer than expected...

Many aristocrats and politicians in Britain and France were full of praise for Mussolini and Hitler when they first came to power. They believed the two dictators would do great things for their countries while being a useful buffer against Communism in the East.

- In 1927 Winston Churchill said to Mussolini, 'If I had been an Italian, I am sure I would have been wholeheartedly with you in your struggle against Leninism.'

- British war minister Alfred Duff Cooper commented after his meeting with the Duce in 1934 that he was 'nicer than expected...we talked chiefly about disarmament and were quite in agreement'.

- There were many aristocratic admirers of the Nazis, including the Duke of Windsor (the former King Edward VIII, who had abdicated in 1936). One rumour suggested that the Nazi minister Hermann Goering had done a deal with the Duke to instal him on the throne once Germany had won the war. Lord Brocket and the Duke of Buccleuch went to Hitler's 50th birthday party, while the Duke of Westminster spent the first year of the war demanding that peace be made with Germany.

- Aristocrat Unity Mitford (whose sister Diana married Oswald Mosley in 1936) was obsessed with the Führer, following him to restaurants and political rallies until he noticed her. Eventually the Führer grew fond of his 'child', as he called Mitford. When England declared war on Germany in September 1939, she was so devastated that she shot herself in the head with a pistol. But the intriguing story that she had a love-child with Hitler is probably untrue.

- Further shenanigans emerged in 2008: in 1940, the British diplomat James Lonsdale-Bryans had travelled to Italy (apparently on his own initiative) to meet with German ambassador Ulrich von Hassell. Lonsdale-Bryans proposed a deal whereby Germany would be given a free rein in Europe, while the British Empire would control the rest of the world. It didn't work out.

Though Japan had invaded Manchuria in northeast China in 1931, the clouds of war really started to gather in 1936, when Germany invaded its former territory in the Rhineland, the border region between Germany and France. It was a huge gamble, but it paid off. As Hitler later admitted, 'If the French had then marched into the Rhineland we would have had to withdraw with our tails between our legs.'

Mussolini had already revealed his hand in 1935, when Italy invaded Abyssinia (now Ethiopia), using bombers, heavy artillery and even poison gas against poorly armed Ethiopian soldiers.

In 1936 Italy and Germany joined forces to help General Franco's Fascists defeat the left-wing government in Spain. The Spanish Civil War gave Hitler the perfect opportunity to try out some of his shiny new weapons: around 100 German bombers formed the Condor Legion, which bombed the Basque town of Guernica on 26 April 1937 – an event which shocked the world and inspired a famous anti-war painting by Pablo Picasso.

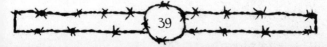

By November 1936, Germany had also signed treaties of friendship with both Italy and Japan. This became a full military alliance in 1939, known as the 'Rome–Berlin–Tokyo Axis', which is why the three countries are often known as the Axis Powers (though there was very little co-operation between Germany and Japan once the war started).

While other nations battled with the Great Depression, Germany, Japan and Italy set about grabbing as much land as they could. The League of Nations, a predecessor of the United Nations, had been set up after World War One to settle disputes peacefully. But, with no armed forces to back up its decisions, it could do little more than squawk in protest.

Things stepped up another gear with the Japanese invasion of China in 1937. Over the next two years, some 800,000 Chinese and 50,000 Japanese died in the fighting, and 50 million Chinese were driven from their homes. Though Japan now controlled the coastline, it couldn't deliver a knock-out blow to the Chinese forces under Chiang Kai-shek.

Which Reich?

The rule of the Nazis, from January 1933 to May 1945, was known as the Third Reich (from the German for 'empire'). Why?

- **The First Reich** was the Holy Roman Empire, the collection of German and neighbouring territories that began in AD 962 when Otto the Great was crowned in Rome. It lasted in one form or another until 1806, when it was defeated by Napoleon.

- **The Second Reich** was created by the 'Iron Chancellor' Prince Otto von Bismarck in 1871, when Germany began to see itself as a unified nation for the first time. It ended when Kaiser Wilhelm II abdicated at the end of World War One.

- Hitler hoped his **Third Reich** would last a thousand years.

- Secret MI5 files reveal Nazi plans for a **'Fourth Reich'**. By planting groups of secret agents in postwar Europe, they hoped to destabilise governments after the end of World War Two. When the time was right, the Nazi party would reappear and create a new German empire.

In Europe, few politicians were bothered by the war in Asia. All eyes were on Hitler, who was clearly determined to turn Germany into a world power. In 1938 the Germans marched unopposed into Austria, an event known as the Anschluss ('union'), after a well-planned coup by the Austrian Nazi party. Later in the year, Hitler claimed the Sudetenland in western Czechoslovakia, which had been German before the Treaty of Versailles. The Aryan race needed more room, he claimed.

> 'The aim of German policy is to ensure the preservation of racial community and to enlarge it. It is, therefore, a question of *Lebensraum* [living space].'

> *Hitler, 5 November 1937*

Yet again Hitler gambled on his opponents backing down. British prime minister Neville Chamberlain claimed Czechoslovakia was 'a far-away country of which we know little' and therefore not worth risking war over. To be fair, Britain was too much in debt to finance an army capable of stopping Germany, and couldn't at this stage rely on support from the United States (which had a tiny army), Russia or France.

Chamberlain flew to Hitler's summer home at Berchtesgaden in the Bavarian Alps, and on 30 September 1938 signed the Munich Agreement which handed the Sudetenland to Germany. The Czechs felt they had been deserted – and they were right. The Nazi secret police were soon rounding up thousands of suspects who might oppose Hitler.

'I got the impression that here was a man who could be relied on when he had given his word.'

Chamberlain on Hitler, 1938

When Chamberlain arrived back in Britain, the streets were lined with cheering crowds wanting to shake his hand. He proudly waved the peace agreement and boasted of 'peace for our time', having believed Hitler's claim that 'I have no more territorial demands to make in Europe.'

It was another one of Hitler's big lies. In March 1939 German troops seized western Czechoslovakia and occupied Prague. Hitler gained more than just territory – entire steel and chemical factories were moved from Czechoslovakia and reassembled in Austria.

Enough is enough

Full-scale war was looking increasingly inevitable as Hitler eyed former German territories in Poland. At this point Britain and France drew a line in the sand. Both promised to declare war if Poland was attacked. Meanwhile Mussolini, miffed that Hitler hadn't told him in advance about Czechoslovakia, decided it was time to grab a piece of the action for himself. The Italians invaded Albania and deposed its king – though, as one Italian official remarked: 'If only the Albanians had possessed a well-armed fire brigade, they could have driven us back into the Adriatic.'

Hitler had ordered German businessmen to drop everything and re-arm the country as quickly as possible. By 1939 the German arms industry accounted for a quarter of the country's economy. This led to a huge labour shortage, despite the extra manpower gained by taking over Austria and Czechoslovakia. The only solution was to find fresh supplies of men and materials from outside the Reich.

Did this push Hitler into full-scale war? Some think so. On 23 May 1939 the Führer assembled 14 senior officers in Berlin and explained that Germany needed a war because the Reich's economy was in such dire straits. A month later, Hermann Goering drew up plans to conscript 7 million men into the armed forces. Prisoners of war, prison inmates and Czech workers would be used as slave labour in German factories and farms.

In the summer of 1939 Britain, France and Russia discussed an alliance, but no firm agreement was reached. Hitler swooped and signed a Non-Aggression Pact with Stalin in August. Now Germany would not have to fight a war on two fronts. The deal took the rest of the world by complete surprise and there was outcry at the Soviets' 'wickedness'.

The ink on the agreement was barely dry when Hitler gave the green light for the invasion of Poland. On 1 September Nazi troops and aircraft flooded into Poland. Ever the gambler, Hitler hoped that Britain and France would still prefer to avoid war. This time he was wrong.

How they lined up

Allies	Axis
Czechoslovakia	Germany
Poland	Japan (1937–45)
France	Italy (1940–43)
British Empire	Hungary (1941–45)
Canada	Romania (1941–44)
Australia	Bulgaria (1941–44)
New Zealand	Thailand (1942–45)
South Africa	Croatia (1941–45)
Soviet Union (1941–45)	
USA (1941–45)	
China (1937–45)	
Yugoslavia (1941–45)	
Greece (1940–45)	
Norway (1940–45)	
Netherlands (1940–45)	
Belgium (1940–45)	
Philippines (1941–45)	
Brazil (1942–45)	
Mexico (1942–45)	

Mexico sent Squadron 201 to the Pacific and eight Mexican pilots were killed in action, while 25,000 Brazilian troops fought in Italy from 1944 to 1945, losing over 900 men.

Soldiers' nicknames

- **British:** Limey (US), Tommy (German), Pongo (RAF – 'Where the army goes, the pong goes').

- **American:** GI, GI Joe, Dogface (US), Yank (British), Ami (German), Kaugummisoldaten (chewing-gum soldiers – Nazi propaganda), Wiederkäuer (cud-chewing animals – also Nazi propaganda).

- **German:** Kraut, Fritz, Jerry (British), Heinie (US/Canadian), Boche, Chleuh, Doryphores (French), Landser, Schütze-Arsch ('soldier's arse' – i.e. lowest of the low – German)

- **Italian:** Eye-tie (British), Goombah (US), Makkaroni or Spaghetti (German)

- **Japanese:** Nip, Jap (US)

- **Russian:** Red/Commie/Ruskie (US), Ivan (German)

- **Australian:** Digger.

> **❛** We are not retreating –
> we are advancing
> in another direction. **❜**

US general Douglas MacArthur

CHAPTER TWO

THE AXIS INVADES

here was no ultimatum or declaration of war. The first shot was fired from the elderly German battleship SMS *Schleswig-Holstein*, which had taken up position opposite the Westerplatte Garrison at Danzig (now Gdańsk), in the early hours of 1 September.

'Germans in Poland are persecuted with bloody terror and driven from their houses... in order to put an end to this lunacy, I have no other choice than to meet force with force from now on.'

Hitler's supposed justification for war, 1 September 1939

The order to fire was given at 4.47 a.m. World War Two had begun, and a Polish soldier, Staff Sergeant Wojciech Nazsarek, became its first casualty. An hour later German aircraft bombed Warsaw and destroyed the bulk of the Polish air force on the ground.

The Germans' *Blitzkrieg* ('lightning war') tactics were brutally effective, sweeping aside the Polish army in just a few days and surrounding the capital Warsaw within a week. Though the Polish army was larger, they found it hard to counter the fast German attacks, as fleeing civilians clogged the roads. Right from the off, the boundary between combatants and civilians was horribly blurred.

There's a persistent myth about Polish cavalry units bravely charging German tanks, but it never happened – the story was made up by Italian journalists.

Operation Canned Goods

Talking to his generals before the war, Hitler declared: 'I shall give a propagandist reason for starting the war. Never mind whether it is plausible or not.' So World War Two was launched with a bizarre stunt, codenamed Operation Canned Goods.

The 'goods' in question were 12 convicts who had been given lethal injections. SS officers dressed their unconscious bodies in Polish clothing, riddled them with bullets, then dumped them outside a German radio station near the Polish border, so it looked as if they had been killed while attacking the station. To complete the deception, Alfred Naujocks, a Polish-speaking German, grabbed the radio station's microphone and broadcast: 'People of Poland, the time has come for war between Poland and Germany!' The next day, members of the press were invited to view the bodies, supposedly evidence that the Poles had attacked first.

After the war Naujocks confessed all at the Nuremburg trials, then sold his story to the media. He was later suspected (but not found guilty) of participating in ODESSA – an organised effort to smuggle SS officers out of the country to avoid prosecution.

Quick as a flash

The good weather of early September 1939 allowed the Germans to try out their new tactic, the *Blitzkrieg*, or 'lightning war':

Step 1: Bombers fly deep into enemy territory, destroying air bases, ammunition dumps, railway stations and military headquarters.

Step 2: Dive-bombers scream down to bomb and machine-gun enemy front-line troops. They also bomb towns to create panic and disruption amongst the civilian population.

Step 3: German tanks, or *Panzers*, and motorised troop carriers look for weak spots in the enemy front line, bursting through to attack strongpoints from behind.

Step 4: The bulk of the army, the foot-sloggers, pour through to mop up any resistance.

Stuka dive-bombers

There was no public outcry in Britain. But there was a feeling in government that it was time to stand up and be counted, as the Conservative Chief Whip explained to MP Henry 'Chips' Channon: 'It must be war, Chips, old boy, there's no other way out.'

On 3 September, Britain – together with its colonies Australia, Canada, New Zealand and India – declared war, dragging its ally France with it. People listened in stunned silence as they heard the news on crackling radios. In the build-up to World War One there had been great enthusiasm among the public. This time around, there were no illusions about what lay ahead. It was more a case of 'Let's get it over with.'

Despite this, the Poles were left to fight alone. If the French had launched an all-out attack in the west, the Germans might have been unable to stop them. Typically, Hitler had gambled most of his forces on the job in hand rather than preparing for a world war. But poor intelligence meant that both Britain and France seriously overestimated the strength of the German forces.

friend or foe?

As in any other war, 'friendly fire', that classic contradiction in terms, played its part from the outset.

- The first time Spitfires fired their guns in anger was on 6 September 1939, when they shot down two planes, killing one of the pilots. Sadly, these were two Hurricanes from another British squadron. At the time, British fighter planes were not fitted with IFF equipment (Identification Friend or Foe), and a radar operator thought he was co-ordinating an attack on enemy planes.

- On 10 September 1939 British submarine HMS *Triton* assumed it had detected a German U-boat, and fired two torpedoes. It sank another British submarine, HMS *Oxley*, killing 52 crew and leaving only two survivors. It was the first Royal Navy vessel sunk in the war.

- On 10 May 1940 three Luftwaffe planes bombed the German town of Freiburg im Breisgau by mistake, killing 57 people. The crews thought they were over the French city of Dijon.

- On 28 June 1940 Marshal Italo Balbo, the Commander-in-Chief of Italian North Africa, was killed by 'friendly fire' while landing in Tobruk, Libya.

- On 23 October 1942, during the battle of El Alamein, fire from British artillery caused over 60 casualties among the 51st (Highland) Infantry Division.

- During the Allied invasion of Sicily, General Omar Bradley's armoured column was attacked by a flight of American A-36 Apache planes. The tanks identified the aircraft as friendly and lit yellow smoke flares, but when the attacks continued, they returned fire and shot down one of the planes. After the pilot parachuted to earth, he was brought in front of Bradley, who fumed: 'You silly sonuvabitch, didn't you see our yellow recognition signals?' To which the pilot replied, 'Oh... is that what it was?'

On 17 September Soviet troops also attacked Poland from the east, playing their part in the secret prewar deal to conquer Poland and divide it with Germany. The Red Army, brutalised by years of oppression under Stalin, went on a bloody rampage. The Soviet secret police rounded up thousands of Polish army officers, who were then shot in the back of the head and buried in a giant pit in the forest of Katyn. Similar massacres of Polish police

officers and intellectuals were also carried out. Prisoners were scalded with boiling water, had their noses, ears, eyes and breasts cut off, or were tied together with barbed wire. Whole families of Poles, Latvians and Lithuanians were sent to Siberian prison camps, where many were worked to death in freezing conditions.

The Germans were no less ruthless. The invasion of Poland saw the first appearance of the notorious SS *Einsatzgruppen* ('task forces') – murder squads set up to find and kill Jews and community leaders such as priests, teachers and aristocrats.

> 'Close your hearts to pity! Act brutally! Eighty million people must obtain what is their right... The stronger man is right... Be harsh and remorseless! Be steeled against all signs of compassion!'
>
> *Hitler to his generals, prior to the invasion of Poland*

The experience of the war in France and Britain was very different. In the weeks after war was declared there was a flurry of activity: ships sailed in convoys, people

carried gas masks in case the Germans dropped gas bombs, some 700,000 children were evacuated from London, and the streets were blacked out at night.

Everyone watched and waited. But very little happened until the spring. These early months were known as the 'phoney war' in Britain, the *drôle de guerre* ('funny war') in France and the *Sitzkrieg* ('sitting war') in Germany. Many British generals and politicians were convinced the Germany economy was about to implode. Again they had been let down by bad intelligence: most Germans were well fed and delighted with the victory in Poland, and a blockade was impossible while Russia was Germany's ally. In Britain, by contrast, rationing had to be introduced early in 1940.

There was nothing phoney about the so-called Winter War in Finland, where some 25,000 Finns and 125,000 Soviets died after Russia launched an attack on 30 November 1939. The Finns held out for over 100 days, but were forced to sign a peace treaty on 12 March 1940 after a Soviet breakthrough.

The War Cup

There were no bombing raids in Britain during the first few months. Over 780 footballers joined the armed services, while others went down the coal mines. Even so, the English Football League decided to start a new competition, the Football League War Cup. The whole competition – 137 games – was squeezed into nine weeks. In May 1940 Hitler invaded France, and in the days leading up to the final, the British Expeditionary Force was evacuated from Dunkirk. Yet the final went ahead on 8 June. Despite the risk of bombing, over 42,300 fans came to Wembley. West Ham United beat Blackburn Rovers 1–0, with the winning goal scored by Sam Small.

Yet again, France and Britain offered little or no help. Meanwhile their generals came up with all sorts of half-baked schemes. The French wanted to create a second front by getting Greece, Turkey and Yugoslavia to attack Austria from the south. When they offered a paltry 50,000 French troops in support, the Balkans unsurprisingly replied 'Non, merci'. Another mad scheme planned to bomb the Baku oil fields near the Caspian Sea.

But there were no precise maps, few French bombers and a shortage of bombs.

Winston Churchill, now back in charge of the Admiralty (he had had the same job in World War One until the disastrous Gallipoli campaign led to a change of government), wanted the Royal Navy to cut off supplies of iron ore from Sweden to Germany by invading the port of Narvik in Norway. He didn't care that Norway was neutral: 'Small nations must not tie their hands when we are fighting for their rights and freedom'. In the event, the Germans got there first.

Hitler heads west

On 9 April 1940 Germany invaded Denmark and Norway. To save lives, the Danish government ordered its army not to fight. In Norway, the Germans hoped Nazi sympathiser Vidkun Quisling would form a new government and simply hand over power. But the Norwegians rejected Quisling and fought on – this time with British and French help – until 9 June, when events in France meant that they were fighting alone.

The Norwegian invasion forced British prime minister Neville Chamberlain to resign. He was replaced by Winston Churchill on 10 May, and the rest, as they say, is history. Churchill proved such an iconic war leader that even 60 years later, in 2002, he was voted the greatest Briton of all time.

> 'You have sat too long here for any good you have been doing. Depart I say, and let us have done with you. In the name of God, go!'
>
> *MP Leo Amery quotes Oliver Cromwell to Neville Chamberlain in a debate on Norway, 7 May 1940*

At the time, this news was overshadowed by reports that German troops were flooding into Belgium and Holland. The German Blitzkrieg had come to western Europe and proved to be just as effective as it was in Poland. Despite help from the British Expeditionary Force (BEF), the two countries fell by the end of May. There were no prizes for guessing who was next in line.

'V' for Victory

In popular legend, the two-fingered salute or V-sign was waved by English and Welsh longbowmen at their French rivals at the Battle of Agincourt in 1415. Before the battle, so the story goes, the French had threatened to cut off the arrow-shooting fingers of any bowmen they killed or captured; the archers made the V-sign to boast that their fingers were still intact.

True or not, the renewed popularity of the gesture during World War Two was due to Victor de Laveleye, a Belgian minister who had fled to London. In January 1941 he suggested using the sign as a symbol for the ultimate Allied victory over the Nazis. Within weeks chalked-up Vs began appearing on walls across Belgium, the Netherlands and northern France. The V was soon plugged in all BBC foreign-language programmes, backed by the two-finger V-sign of Prime Minister Winston Churchill (sometimes with a cigar between the fingers).

The BBC based its aural V-sign on the opening notes of Beethoven's Fifth Symphony, whose rhythm happens to match the signal for V in Morse code. Its *tat-tat-tat-tat* rhythm, 'knocking on the door' of Nazi Germany, became a call-sign for all broadcasts to occupied countries.

The French were confident that the powerful defences of the Maginot Line could halt any German attack. Instead, one million men and 1,500 tanks bypassed the Line and attacked unexpectedly through the wooded, mountainous Ardennes region. (When the plans were first revealed, they provoked a storm of protest from the majority of German generals. Not for the last time, they were ignored by Hitler.)

Supported by the German air force, the Luftwaffe, German tanks swept on (using accurate French road maps published by Michelin), surrounding towns in pincer movements. The panzer charge was led by General Heinz Guderian, earning him the nickname 'Fast Heinz' among his troops. German Stuka dive-bombers terrified civilians and poorly trained conscripts alike, with loud 'screamers' fitted to both planes and bombs. Meanwhile most German infantry moved as they had always done, on foot. Supported by supplies in horse-drawn carts, many marched an astounding 105 km a day during the first week of the invasion.

The mighty Maginot Line

During World War One, the French belief in
élan ('impetus', or constant attack) resulted
in heavy casualties as lines of soldiers were
mown down by machine guns or blown up by
shells. Next time around, the French were
going to rely on defence. In the 1930s they
built the Maginot Line, a string of
underground forts 140 km long. In reality the
line consisted of 500 separate buildings based
around large forts (ouvrages) 15 km or so apart
which were protected by thick reinforced steel
capable of taking a direct hit from most known
artillery fire.

Though the French army was as big as the
German Wehrmacht, and had more tanks, it
was soon beaten back. After achieving a
breakthrough at Sedan, the German forces
reached the English Channel in a week,
cutting the Allied armies in two. Those in the
north, including many British troops, retreated
into a narrow pocket around Dunkirk
(Dunkerque), a port on the French coast.

The Allied Forces were now at Hitler's mercy,
but incredibly, he ordered a halt – prompted

partly by the boasts of Hermann Goering, head of the Luftwaffe, that his planes would wipe out enemy forces on their own. The delay gave time for a remarkable rescue operation. A force of Royal Navy ships was dispatched, but Dunkirk's docks were too badly damaged to use and the large ships were too big to get close to the beaches. On 27 May 1940 a call went out to small-boat owners: 'Help the Navy.'

Motor boats, trawlers, lifeboats, paddle-steamers and many other types of craft took part in Operation Dynamo. Sunken ships were everywhere. On the beach, thousands of soldiers waited in long queues. German dive-bombers screamed out of the sky and whole ships burst into flames. Amid the chaos, the fleet of small boats bravely ferried troops who were queuing in the water to larger craft further out to sea.

Over nine days, some 226,000 British and 110,000 French, Dutch and Belgian troops were picked up (though they were forced to leave behind some 63,000 vehicles – including all their tanks – 2,472 artillery pieces and

90,000 rifles). In Britain the evacuation was hailed as a miracle. Hitler was equally delighted by the British departure, decreeing that German bells should ring for three days and nights to celebrate the victory. The French were rather less rapturous. To them Dunkirk was a betrayal, as the French soldiers were evacuated only after all the British troops had been taken off the beaches. Around 150,000 French soldiers were left behind and became POWs.

The Germans pushed on towards Paris and captured it on 14 June, marching down the Champs Elysées just a month after invading. On 22 June France surrendered to the Nazis. This astonishing victory, achieved with the loss of just 27,000 German dead, was Hitler's greatest military triumph.

The Führer insisted that the French surrender be signed in the same railway carriage that had been used for the German surrender at the end of World War One. Revenge was sweet for the man who wore his nickname, 'The Corporal' (his rank during the previous war), as a badge of honour.

franglais spoken here?

Despite having left the French army in the lurch at Dunkirk, the British were desperate to keep France in the war. Far-fetched schemes were proposed to turn Brittany into a great fortress or to force the United States into the war. There were also demands for all French ships to sail to British ports so they wouldn't fall into German hands.

In a last roll of the dice, Churchill and General de Gaulle rang the French premier, Paul Reynaud, on 16 June 1940, suggesting that Britain and France become one united nation. The proposal caused an uproar in the French Cabinet. Reynaud was forced to resign and a new government was formed late that night under a hero of the First World War, Marshal Philippe Pétain. Pétain immediately negotiated an armistice with Germany.

France was now divided in two. Germany controlled the north while Pétain's puppet French government, based at Vichy in the Auvergne, was left in charge of southern and eastern France. Even in 'unoccupied' France,

the German secret police, or Gestapo, were everywhere. Their ruthless brutality only encouraged the growing Resistance movement. Meanwhile General Charles de Gaulle, the leader of the 'Free French', fled to England with, at first, only a modest number of supporters.

> 'France has lost a battle.
> She has not lost the war'.

General Charles de Gaulle, still optimistic after the fall of France in June 1940

Churchill decided to help the French Resistance, or Maquis, by setting up the Special Operations Executive (SOE) in July 1940. His aim was to 'set Europe ablaze', chiefly by sabotaging factories, ammunition dumps, railway lines and anything else that could help the German war effort. Some 60 training schools were set up for SOE agents, while secret laboratories invented a range of gadgets from concealed maps to silencers. By the end of the war some 11,000 agents had been trained. It was very dangerous work: of 392 agents sent into France, at least 104 were killed.

Resistance...

In occupied Europe, thousands chose to resist the Germans and Italians. Not all resistance involved dramatic explosions or ambushes. 'Go slows' at work, deliberate 'red tape', the hiding of Jews or other fugitives, and small-scale sabotage all played their part.

- The largest resistance armies were the 142,000 or so Soviet and Polish guerrillas based in the Pinsk Marshes, between Belarus and the Ukraine. Their hit-and-run raids against German supply lines infuriated the Nazis so much that they even planned to drain thousands of square kilometres of marshland. Between February and July 1943 the partisans destroyed 44 railway bridges and 298 locomotives.

- A partisan army led by Tito (real name: Josip Broz) was particularly successful. By 1944, Tito had taken over much of northwest Yugoslavia. However, a million Yugoslavs died as a result of infighting with a rival partisan group, the Chetniks.

- In Germany, a student movement known as the White Rose handed out leaflets calling for opposition to Hitler's regime. The leaders of the movement, Hans and Sophie Scholl, Christoph Probst, Alexander Schmorell, Kurt Huber and Willi Graf, were executed by guillotine in 1943.

- The Nazis reacted viciously to resistance activities, usually working on the basis of 100 executions for every German soldier killed. In Operation Anthropoid, a British-trained Czech assassin killed SS security chief Reinhard Heydrich, the 'Butcher of Prague', by hurling a grenade at him. In retaliation, the Nazis arrested 13,000 people and wiped out the village of Lidice.

- The Nazis were relentless in their pursuit of suspects. Their famous 'Red Poster' plastered onto the walls of Paris in April 1944 showed the faces of ten partisans they had killed earlier that year.

- Many partisans were equally ruthless. Recruits thought to be traitors were shot along with their families, and their homes were burnt to the ground as a warning to others who might have been bribed by the Germans.

...or collaboration?

Collaboration by civilians ranged from survival (doing the laundry to earn extra food for your family) to helping out in massacres organised by the SS murder squads, or Einsatzgruppen.

- **Russia:** In September 1941 Ukrainian police officers helped in the slaughter of over 33,000 Jews at Babi Yar near Kiev.

- **Poland:** Collaborators in Polish towns helped the Soviet secret police, the NKVD, to hunt down Polish army officers, police and other 'enemies' in hiding.

- **France:** Some 7,500 Frenchmen formed the Charlemagne Division of the Waffen SS. They fought so well on the Eastern Front that many were awarded the Iron Cross for their bravery. They were also among the last defenders of Hitler's bunker in May 1945.

  After the war, French women who had fallen in love with German soldiers had their hair hacked off and swastikas were painted on them with mud.

- **Britain:** The British Free Corps was made up of British POWs who had been recruited by the Nazis. In the end, fewer than 60 men signed up and the unit was more of a propaganda tool than an effective fighting force.

Notorious collaborators

- **Britain:** William Joyce, nicknamed Lord Haw-Haw, was an American-born Fascist who broadcast Nazi propaganda to Britain. After the war he was hanged for treason by the British.

- **Norway:** Vidkun Quisling, a Norwegian politician, served as Minister-President of Norway under the Nazis from 1942 to 1945 and helped in the deportation of Jews. During the war, the word *quisling* became synonymous with 'traitor'. He was tried in Norway after the war and executed by firing squad on 24 October 1945.

- **France:** Maurice Papon, a former French cabinet minister, was convicted in 1998, after a marathon trial, of helping Nazis to deport Jews to concentration camps.

A recent biography claims that French fashion designer Coco Chanel was a Nazi spy, codenamed Westminster. She spent most of the war staying at the Hôtel Ritz in Paris, a favourite haunt of Nazi generals and ministers such as Hermann Goering and Joseph Goebbels.

The Battle of Britain

'The battle for France is over. The whole fury and might of the enemy must very soon be turned on us... The Battle of Britain is about to begin.'

Winston Churchill, 18 June 1940

Having conquered France, Hitler now turned his attention to Britain. The date for the invasion, codenamed Operation Sealion, was set for 15 September 1940. But without control of the skies, his armies couldn't cross the English Channel in safety.

The Battle of Britain, which began on 10 July, was the first battle fought solely in the air. In the first phase, German planes attacked convoy ships in the Channel, hoping to lure in British fighter planes and destroy them. German air chief Hermann Goering bragged that he could defeat the RAF in just four days.

In August the Germans switched tactics and attacked airfields and aircraft factories. Several airfields, such as Biggin Hill, were flattened. If the Germans had stuck with these tactics, the battle might have swung in their favour. But when the RAF bombed Berlin on 25 August, Hitler was furious and ordered an immediate retaliation.

On 7 September more than 1,000 German bombers and fighters attacked London, killing 430 people in the East End. The 'Blitz' had begun. For the next eight months, up to 160 German bombers rained bombs on the capital, night after night, dropping a total of 18,000 tonnes of high explosive. When Buckingham Palace took a direct hit, the Queen proudly said: 'Now we can look the East End in the face.' Other cities suffered too, especially Coventry, and during the war German bombs claimed some 40,000 civilian lives.

At first British cities were poorly protected, but by 1941 the RAF had radar-equipped planes, better searchlights and accurate anti-aircraft guns. Air Raid Wardens, fire and ambulance crews worked flat out to deal with the carnage. Civilians took cover in air-raid shelters, but were safest in the London Tube stations deep below ground.

Operation Willi

In July 1940 the Nazis hatched a plan to kidnap the Duke of Windsor (the former King Edward VIII), who was believed to be an admirer of the Führer. Hitler sent his SS intelligence chief, Walter Schellenberg, to Spain, where the Duke was on holiday. His mission was to lure the Duke to Germany with a bribe of 50 million Swiss francs. If this failed, Edward was to be kidnapped. While a cautious Schellenberg hesitated, Britain got wind of the plot and had the Duke removed to a more secure haven in the Bahamas, where he spent the rest of the war.

Even in underground stations, Londoners were still at risk. On 14 October 1940 an armour-piercing bomb penetrated 10 metres underground and exploded just above the cross passage between the two platforms at Balham tube station. Most of the 66 casualties were caused by the blast or by flying debris, but stories soon circulated of people drowned in the rising waters after sewage pipes burst.

The bombing raids on cities at least gave the RAF time to repair its airfields and train new pilots. They also developed new tactics such as the 'Big Wing', in which hundreds of fighters joined forces to attack the incoming German bombers.

Radio Direction Finding (RDF) stations on the coastline detected incoming planes and avoided the need for endless patrols, while planes such as the Hurricane and Spitfire could outfly many Luftwaffe bombers and fighters. The mounting casualties forced the Luftwaffe to switch to night raids, and it carried out its last mass raid on 15 September (now Battle of Britain Day).

Reach for the Sky

'Big Wing' tactics were first used by planes under Douglas Bader's command. Bader had lost both his legs in an air accident in 1931, but was able to fly again with a pair of artificial legs. Shot down in 1941, he made several escape attempts from German prison camps. In 1956 his story was made into a film, *Reach for the Sky*, though it glossed over the fact that the real-life Bader swore constantly.

Though smaller raids continued until 16 May 1941, the RAF had won the real Battle of Britain, forcing Hitler to shelve his invasion plans. But only just: during August and September, when the battle was at its height, Fighter Command lost 832 fighters, the Luftwaffe only 668. Nonetheless, it was a remarkable victory.

> 'Never in the field of human conflict has so much been owed by so many to so few.'
>
> *Winston Churchill commenting on the RAF's role in the Battle of Britain, September 1940*

Wish you were here?

In the past 70 years scores of novels, plays, films and documentaries have explored what might have happened if the Germans had successfully invaded Britain. In 2010, however, the real plans for the assault were discovered in a 446-page Nazi briefing book:

- Postcards identifying landmarks such as Land's End and the piers at Brighton were given to German troops.

- Large colour maps showed the whole of the south coast.

- Six divisions of German troops would land in Kent, another four in Sussex and Hampshire, and a final three divisions would attack Dorset.

- Shock troops would attempt to capture the docks at Dover, followed by the main force.

- Invasion techniques were practised on the beaches of France in September and early October 1940 – but RAF bombing raids in December destroyed most of the invasion barges at Dunkirk.

New fronts

The conflict raging in Europe soon spread to North Africa. On 3 July 1940, after the Germans had overrun France, the British Royal Navy attacked French warships at Mers-el-Kebir in Algeria, sinking a battleship and damaging five others. It then launched a bold night attack on the Italian navy at Taranto in Sicily, sinking several Italian warships with torpedoes launched from ancient Swordfish biplanes. This gave the British control of the Mediterranean, which they needed to protect the Suez Canal route to India and the oilfields of the Middle East.

'The Mediterranean will be turned
into an Italian lake.'

*Benito Mussolini, planning a new
Roman Empire*

Though Italy had declared war on 10 June 1940, Mussolini slyly waited until the French forces had all but collapsed before committing his troops to an attack on southern France. Even so, the Italian dictator was eager to prove to Hitler that he could match the

German successes. So, in August 1940, Italian troops launched an attack on the British colony of Somaliland (now part of Somalia), which they held for nearly a year.

In October 1940 Mussolini's troops invaded Greece; the Greek army, experienced at fighting in the mountains, repelled the Italians with ease. A month earlier an Italian invasion of Egypt from Libya had failed when its tanks ran out of petrol 100 km over the border. A small British force under General Archibald Wavell counter-attacked in December. After defeating Italian forces at Sidi Barani it took the vital stronghold of Tobruk by 22 January, in the meantime capturing 115,000 Italian prisoners and destroying thousands of tanks while suffering few casualties.

The Allies made the most of Wavell's victory: the February issue of *Life* magazine included a story entitled: 'Mussolini Takes a Bad Licking in Africa.' Behind the scenes things were less rosy – Britain was now almost bankrupt. US president Franklin D. Roosevelt came to the rescue, proclaiming that the United States would be the 'Arsenal of Democracy'.

From 11 March 1941 the US Lend-Lease Act ensured a steady flow of arms and food to Britain and the Soviet Union. By the end of the war some $50 billion of supplies had been shipped. Roosevelt wanted to keep Britain afloat until the United States entered the war. In return, the United States swallowed up Britain's gold reserves and overseas investments. This agreement, along with the cost of the war, effectively finished Britain as a world power.

To bail out Mussolini, German forces arrived in North Africa in February 1941 to defend Libya from the British. Then on 6 April the Germans invaded Greece and Yugoslavia. Though Yugoslavia fell quickly, hundreds of thousands of soldiers vanished into the mountains, and for the rest of the war these partisans tied down huge numbers of German troops.

The Greek forces, despite British support, were overwhelmed by the invading Germans, and by 27 April Athens had fallen. The conquest was complete with the capture of Crete on 1 June. The British had planned to

use the island as a base for bombing raids. But, just after dawn on 20 May 1941, as many of the Allied soldiers stationed on the island were finishing breakfast, the air above was suddenly filled with hundreds of German transport aircraft and parachutes. Some 20,000 German paratroopers began to descend from the sky. They captured the island in just 10 days, but at a heavy price – one general described Crete as 'the graveyard of the German paratroopers'. Hitler forbade further airborne invasions.

The key British base in the Mediterranean was now the tiny island of Malta. Field Marshal Erwin Rommel, in command of Axis forces in North Africa, warned that: 'Without Malta the Axis will end by losing control of North Africa.' The Axis forces decided to starve the island into submission. It was defended by just three old Gladiator biplanes, nicknamed *Faith*, *Hope* and *Charity*. They were no match for the Luftwaffe, which dropped twice as many bombs on Malta as it had on London. By August 1941 many on the island were starving, but soon after the attacks eased off and the expected German invasion never

happened – though the British did suffer a major blow when the German submarine *U-81* sank its largest aircraft carrier, HMS *Ark Royal*, as it ferried more planes to defend Malta.

Mysterious Minister Hess

On 24 May 1941 Rudolf Hess, the Nazi party secretary, parachuted into Scotland, bailing out of his plane after a 1,500-kilometre solo flight. His mission: to negotiate a truce with the British. Hess surrendered to a farmer named David McClean, who was armed with a pitchfork. After being offered tea at McClean's cottage he was taken into custody. Hitler disowned Hess, saying he was insane. Was he right? Or was Hess hoping that a dramatic coup would bring him back into favour with the Führer?

No-one seems to know for sure. The British imprisoned Hess in the Tower of London, and after the war he was sentenced at Nuremburg to life imprisonment at Spandau prison in Berlin. Officially Hess killed himself in 1987, aged 93, though rumours abounded that the body was a double and the real Rudolf Hess had been murdered years before by British secret agents.

The biggest gamble of all

Throughout this period Hitler toyed with the idea of invading Egypt and the Middle East. But he had bigger fish to fry. Despite his pact with Stalin in 1939, Hitler had always planned to attack the Soviet Union. The German invasion of Russia, codenamed Operation Barbarossa, began on 22 June 1941. Hitler was so sure of victory, he didn't even ask Japan to launch a co-ordinated attack in the East (partly because he didn't want to share the spoils). In the end, Barbarossa proved to be his greatest gamble – one that eventually lost him the war.

'You only have to kick in the door and the whole rotten structure will come crashing down.'

Adolf Hitler on invading the Soviet Union

There was much to gain: the wheatfields of the Ukraine, the oil of the Caucasus and the destruction of the hateful Communist Party. Hitler planned to kill some 150 million Russians he regarded as *Untermenschen* (subhumans), then enslave the rest. According to Heinrich Himmler, head of the SS, these

Russian slaves would need to know just three things: how to count to ten in German, write their name, and know their master. In the event, the Germans murdered 10 million civilians along with 2 million POWs. It was the biggest, bloodiest campaign of the war.

Three German army groups – over 4 million soldiers if you include Italians and Romanians, along with 600,000 vehicles and 750,000 horses – headed for Leningrad (now St Petersburg), Moscow and the Ukraine. Using Blitzkrieg tactics, they advanced quickly. In some regions, such as Latvia and Lithuania, there was such hatred of the Communists that the Germans were welcomed at first – but not for long.

Stalin took days to get over the shock. He had dismissed reports of the German build-up as a dastardly British attempt to drag Russia into the war. As a result, a large chunk of the Soviet Air Force was blown away in the first three days, while hundreds of thousands of Russian soldiers were encircled by the Germans in a pocket between Minsk and the Polish border. Fearing a revolt among his own ministers, Stalin came close to a breakdown. In time, the dictator got the hang of listening to his advisers, but the learning process cost millions of Russian lives.

Within three weeks German troops were at the River Dnieper and ready to take Kiev. It all seemed so easy. Hitler rubbed his hands in glee and forecast victory in Moscow by the end of August. But the Russians were not ready to roll over, and as German supply lines became overstretched, the enormity of the task ahead became clear to Hitler's generals.

On 3 July Stalin proclaimed the 'Great Patriotic War'. His troops responded by fighting to the death, and though his pleas for British support fell on deaf ears, he soon had another ally in the weather. Heavy rains in August and September bogged down the advancing German troops, while partisan groups behind the lines harried the German supply lines.

Put simply, the Germans forgot two important things. The first was the sheer size of the Russian army. More than 2.4 million Soviet

troops had been captured by December 1941, but in the month of October alone the Soviets put together 11 new armies once it became clear that there was no threat from Japan.

'The Red Army and Navy and the whole Soviet people must fight for every inch of Soviet soil, fight to the last drop of blood for our towns and villages... onward, to victory!'

Josef Stalin, emulating Churchill, July 1941

The second factor was the size of the country itself – so enormous that it simply swallowed up the invaders. In France, the German armies grew closer as they advanced. In Russia, they spread further and further apart. Many roads were little more than dirt tracks, and while Hitler and his generals debated whether to push on towards Moscow or attack on the wings, the roads turned to gloop in the rain. The German armies, supplied largely by horse-drawn wagons, came to a standstill.

By early September the city of Leningrad, a vital stronghold, was under siege. After an initial attack failed, the Germans tried to starve the city into surrender. In desperation, the inhabitants began to eat cats, dogs, grass –

and even, it is claimed, each other. With the approach of winter the streets were covered in dead bodies, as it was impossible to bury them in the frozen ground. When spring came, the bodies thawed and rotted, spreading disease. But Leningrad held on, and a concert was even performed inside the Philharmonic Hall by musicians recalled from the front line. It included a piece written for the occasion by the famous Russian composer Dmitri Shostakovich.

The Russian capital, Moscow, was also under attack by the end of the year. The Soviet secret police opened fire to keep panicking crowds under control as they fled the capital in their millions. But the bitter Russian winter crippled the Germans, who were supplied only with summer clothing. (Their Italian colleagues fared even worse, as their boots were fitted with cardboard soles that disintegrated in the snow, forcing them to steal boots from dead Russians.) Meanwhile supplies were running low, and the troops were worn out from four months of combat.

Dobbin, Rudolph and Dumbo go to war

It wasn't only humans who gave their all for the war effort:

- **Horses and mules:** For all the talk of 'lightning war', the Germans used over two and a half million horses and mules (and the Red Army almost three million) to transport supplies. Many armies also had cavalry units for scouting, especially on the vast plains of Russia. There were some 10,000 mules in the US army. Sure-footed and patient, they could pick their way along the most treacherous mountain track or find a path through the thickest jungle.

- **Reindeer:** During the Winter War of 1939–40, the Finns used 100,000 reindeer to carry supplies and wounded, and even for patrols.

- **Camels:** Camel cavalry, or *méharistes*, were used by the French in North Africa.

- **Elephants:** Gyles Mackrell, a 53-year-old tea planter, saved 200 Burmese refugees from the advancing Japanese army by using a team of elephants to carry them across a mountain pass and rivers swollen by the monsoon rains.

- **Dogs:** Many civilians donated their dogs to the war effort. Perhaps the most famous war dog was Chips, who served with the US Infantry in North Africa, Sicily, Italy, France and Germany. During the invasion of Sicily, Chips and his handler were pinned down on the beach by an Italian machine-gun team. Chips jumped into the pillbox and, despite being wounded, forced the crew to run out and surrender to US troops. He survived the war and was returned to the family in New York that had donated him.

- **Pigeons:** Still considered a valuable asset on the battlefield, there were over 54,000 military pigeons serving in the US Army Signal Corps.

- **Cats:** After the sinking of the German battleship *Bismarck* on 18 May 1941, British sailors rescued a black and white cat which they named Oscar. Later in the war, the same cat was on board HMS *Cossack* when it sank and on HMS *Ark Royal* when it went down. Now nicknamed 'Unsinkable Sam', it survived the war and died in 1955.

- **Insects:** Both sides planned to drop Colorado beetles to munch on enemy crops, while Unit 731, Japan's biological warfare unit, used plague-infected fleas and flies covered with cholera to infect the population in China. The insects were sprayed by low-flying aircraft and the resulting epidemics led to the death of 500,000 people.

Ignoring his generals, who insisted their men could not go on, Hitler demanded 'a final effort of willpower'. But German troops were cold and exhausted. As temperatures dropped, the mud turned to concrete. It froze onto wheels and tracks and had to be laboriously chipped off.

The Russians, meanwhile, fought with ever-increasing ferocity. The invasion had united the country as never before. To ensure a steady supply of new weapons, hundreds of factories were shipped lock, stock and barrel to a new industrial zone far to the east behind the Ural mountains. One giant plant took 8,000 railway wagons to move it, but was up and running within four months.

On 6 December the Soviets counterattacked on the outskirts of Moscow. For the first time in the war, the German armies retreated. By the New Year, Moscow was saved. Incensed, Hitler decided to take command of the army himself. With each defeat Hitler listened less to his generals, and became ever more obsessed with his crusade to wipe out the Jews and Slavs.

Uncle Sam joins in

In August 1941 Churchill and Roosevelt met on board the USS *Augusta*, moored off the coast of Newfoundland. When they first came face to face, both men were silent for a moment. Churchill spoke first: 'At long last, Mr President,' to which Roosevelt replied, 'Glad to have you aboard, Mr Churchill.' Five days later they had drafted an agreement that set their goals for the coming years. Known later as the Atlantic Charter, this pledged 'the final destruction of Nazi tyranny'. But there was a long way to go.

On the other side of world, Japan had been carving out an Eastern empire since 1937. Thanks to a modernisation programme that had started in the 1870s, it was now the most developed country in the Pacific. By 1940 it felt strong enough to take on European countries such as Britain, France and the Netherlands, which all had rich colonies in Asia.

When Japan moved into French Indochina (present-day Vietnam, Cambodia and Laos),

Roosevelt froze all Japanese assets in the United States, effectively halting American oil shipments to Japan. When the Netherlands and Britain followed suit, Japan was in real danger of running out of oil. To the Japanese military, a withdrawal from China was completely unacceptable. The only alternative was to tackle the Americans head on.

General Hideki Tojo, the Japanese prime minister, hoped to knock out the United States fleet with a lightning strike, to stop it interfering in Japanese plans to conquer an Asian empire. On 22 November 1941 a Japanese Navy force of six aircraft carriers secretly set sail, under cover of bad weather, until it was within 500 km of Pearl Harbor, Hawaii – the largest American naval base in the Pacific.

On 7 December 1941, 353 Japanese fighters, bombers and torpedo planes took off in two waves. In a few hours, aided by midget submarines, they had sunk 18 US warships, destroyed 188 planes and killed 2,400 Americans (over 1,000 were killed in a single explosion aboard the USS *Arizona*).

The attack came as an almighty shock to the Americans, who declared war the next day on both Japan and Germany. There had been no formal warning, though various conspiracy theories contend that both Churchill and Roosevelt knew about the attack and kept quiet about it so that America would be forced to go to war. British agents had suspected a sneak Japanese attack, but they thought it would be heading the other way, against the Philippines or Malaya.

Underhand it may have been, but the attack on Pearl Harbor was brilliantly planned and executed. That said, the Japanese, fearing a counterattack, had left Pearl Harbor's fuel depot, docks and submarine base intact. Meanwhile America's aircraft carriers, battle-winners in the Pacific war, were safe at sea.

Pearl Harbor changed the entire war. Britain and Russia now had a giant, powerful ally in the battle against the Axis forces. In 1940 the Americans had already decided on 'Plan Dog'. This made defeating the Nazis in Europe a priority, while keeping the Japanese fleet out of the eastern Pacific. The first American

troops arrived in England in January 1942. They were followed by some 1.5 million Americans between July 1943 and June 1944 – 'overpaid, oversexed and over here', as the gripe went.

Another popular joke said there was so much American chewing gum tossed into the fountains of London's Trafalgar Square that the pigeons there were laying rubber eggs. But many locals warmed to the new arrivals who generously flung chocolate bars and gum out of passing trucks to goggle-eyed children. The glamorous GIs were popular with the ladies, too – some 60,000 British women eventually became American war brides.

Car, courtesy Capone

After the attack at Pearl Harbor, President Roosevelt searched for a bulletproof car. But as government regulations put a ban on spending more than $750, the only one available was Al Capone's limo, which had been seized by the Treasury Department after the gangster was arrested for tax evasion. Roosevelt quipped: 'I hope Mr Capone won't mind.'

Short and sharp

During the attack on Pearl Harbor, Mitsuo Fuchida, the Japanese captain who co-ordinated the raid, uttered the code message 'Tora! Tora! Tora!' to show the attack had been a success. Other infamous messages from the war include:

- **'Praise the lord and pass the ammunition'**, credited to Chaplain William A. McGuire during the Pearl Harbor attack. The phrase was later made into a hit song.

- **'Scratch one flat-top'** is how Commander Robert Dixon signalled a successful attack on the Japanese aircraft carrier *Shoho*.

- **'Sighted sub, sank same.'** Ensign Donald Mason's one-sentence radio message after sinking a German U-boat on 28 January 1942.

- **'No armed Englishman remains on the Continent.'** General Gerd von Rundstedt's words to Hitler after the disastrous Allied commando raid on Dieppe was beaten back on 19 August 1942.

- **'*Sturgeon* no longer virgin.'** US Commander W. L. Wright's message after his submarine the USS *Sturgeon* torpedoed its first Japanese ship on 22 January 1942.

- **'There are no atheists in foxholes.'** A line attributed to Lieutenant-Colonel William

Casey but probably made up by US journalist Ernie Pyle.

- 'To hell with Roosevelt, to hell with Babe Ruth, to hell with Roy Acuff.' An insult yelled by Japanese soldiers to US GIs. Babe Ruth was a famous baseball player, while Acuff was the king of Country music.

- 'Tulta munille!' If you believe Väinö Linna's novel *The Unknown Soldier*, this was a Finnish battle cry during World War Two. A rough translation is: 'Fire at their balls!'

- 'There's no land behind the Volga River!' Russian soldiers hollered this as they attacked during the Battle of Stalingrad, summing up their do-or-die attitude. Another slogan was **Za Stalina, za Rodinu** ('For Stalin, for the Motherland').

- 'Tally-ho' was spoken by RAF fighter pilots over their intercoms as they spotted an enemy plane and plunged in for the kill. This strange phrase probably has its origins in fox-hunting, as many of the young pilots at the beginning of the war came from the upper-middle classes for whom hunting was a popular pastime.

'December 7, 1941 –
a date that will live in infamy.'

*US president Franklin D. Roosevelt,
8 December 1941*

The Pacific war was on. The day after Pearl Harbor, 8 December, the Japanese made clear their plans for the rest of Asia by invading the British colony of Malaya (now part of Malaysia). A week later they attacked Burma. As the British retreated, some 600,000 refugees fled west to Bengal; as many as 80,000 of them died on the way. Across Asia, British forces left the locals to fend for themselves, and the abandonment of its colonies dealt a hefty blow to British prestige in the region.

In six months Japan had conquered most of the Asian Pacific seaboard and threatened Australia and India. It also launched an assault on American bases in the Philippines, wiping out the US Far East Air Force in just a few days. The US forces under General Douglas MacArthur were forced to retreat, and on 12 March 1942 MacArthur himself escaped to Australia. On his arrival, the

general came up with his famous catchphrase, 'I shall return,' which was later printed on cigarettes, sweets and matches delivered to Filipino guerillas. And, true to his word, he did.

In 1942 Japanese forces charged into Borneo, Java and Sumatra. The British base of Singapore fell quickly in February. Around 25,000 prisoners were captured, many of whom died later in Japanese camps. In a remarkably short time the Japanese had created a sprawling empire. Through slogans such as 'Asia for the Asians!' the Japanese promoted the idea that they were throwing off the yoke of European imperialism. In Burma they were even welcomed as liberators by thousands of young nationalists.

The grim reality of the so-called Greater East Asia Co-Prosperity Sphere was rather different. In the Philippines an estimated 1 in 20 people died during the Japanese occupation, and when Singapore fell at least 70,000 Chinese people were massacred. In China itself, Japanese troops were instructed to 'Kill all, burn all and loot all.' Rape was a

standard terror tactic, and as many as 100,000 young girls across Asia were forced into becoming 'comfort women' for Japanese soldiers.

In the summer of 1942 General Tojo seemed unstoppable, thanks to the might of the Japanese Navy and the ferocity of his soldiers. But, like Hitler, he was taking a huge gamble. Despite its alliance with Germany and Italy, Japan was effectively on its own.

Conquering an empire was one thing; holding on to it would prove far harder, especially once the vast American war machine swung into action.

'I fear we have only succeeded in awakening a sleeping tiger.'

Japanese admiral Isoruku Yamamoto after the Pearl Harbor raid

Kilroy was here

During World War Two a curious cartoon cropped up all over the world at truck stops, restaurants and military barracks. Accompanied by the phrase 'Kilroy was here', it showed a curious little man with a bald head peering over a fence that hid everything except his eyes and his long nose.

It was found on the torch of the Statue of Liberty, the Arc de Triomphe in Paris and the Marco Polo Bridge in China. US Air Force crews competed to beat Kilroy to isolated places around the world.

According to one legend, during the meeting of the Big Three war leaders in Potsdam, Germany, in July 1945, US president Harry S. Truman, British prime minister Clement Attlee and Stalin shared a luxurious marble bathroom. During the summit an excited Stalin appeared from the bathroom muttering in Russian to one of his staff. A translator overheard Stalin ask: 'Who is Kilroy?'

The most likely origin of the phrase is James J. Kilroy, a welding inspector at the Bethlehem Steel shipyard in Quincy, Massachusetts, who marked his welding work with the words 'Kilroy was here.' This became a common sight around the shipyard, so the story goes, and was imitated by other shipyard workers sent around the world.

The tide turns

The war raged in Africa as well as Asia. In the spring of 1941 Hitler sent his Afrika Korps to help defend the Italian colonies of Libya and Ethiopia against British attack. The German forces were led by Field Marshal Erwin Rommel, a skilled commander nicknamed the 'Desert Fox'. Rommel was highly regarded by both sides for his professionalism and humane treatment of prisoners; he is said to have refused orders to kill Jewish POWs. After capturing the British base at Tobruk and pushing British forces back to the Egyptian border, Rommel threatened to conquer all of North Africa, including the Suez Canal, which was a vital sea route to India.

Churchill was so concerned that he made the long journey to Egypt himself to size up the situation. The British 8th Army was given a new commander, General Bernard Montgomery. After stockpiling vast quantities of weapons and ammunition for six weeks, on 23 October 1941 'Monty' launched a massive counterattack at the battle of El Alamein. The German lines were heavily defended, but the

Allied 900-gun bombardment was so ferocious that it gave the German general Georg Stumme a fatal heart attack.

At first the British troops made slow progress, picking their way through the 'devil's gardens' of anti-tank mines and booby traps. But by 4 November they had broken through the German lines, forcing them into a long retreat westwards. Winston Churchill, convinced that the battle of El Alamein marked the turning point in the war, ordered the ringing of church bells all over Britain.

> 'Now this is not the end. It is not even the beginning of the end. But it is, perhaps, the end of the beginning.'
>
> *Churchill, November 1942*

Further Allied landings in Morocco and Algeria meant that Rommel was now fighting a war on two fronts. After losing the Battle for Tunis, the Afrika Korps surrendered in May 1943. The war for North Africa had been won, and the Allies looked to invade Italy.

A major factor in the Allied success in North Africa was the arrival of arms and equipment from America, such as the Sherman and Grant tanks. In 1942 both the United States and the Soviet Union began to produce a mass of weapons that would eventually win the war and leave them as the two rival superpowers.

Though Japan was at the height of her power in spring 1942, the Americans were ready to fight back. When Japan tried to invade New Guinea the Americans were waiting in ambush, thanks to US codebreakers who had cracked the Japanese naval communications code. At the Battle of the Coral Sea, on 4–8 May, the three US aircraft carriers that had escaped the destruction at Pearl Harbor were put to good use. It was the first naval battle in history in which neither side's ships actually saw or fired on each other. All the fighting took place in the air, and though both sides had heavy losses the Japanese advance was halted.

A month later, on 4 June, the two sides clashed again at Midway Atoll, a stepping stone to Hawaii. The Japanese hoped to lure the United States' aircraft carriers into a trap, but again the Americans were waiting in

ambush. In the space of a few minutes US planes destroyed four Japanese carriers and a cruiser, dealing a stunning blow to the Japanese fleet. From this point on the Japanese struggled to replace their ships and aircrews, while American forces grew ever stronger.

On the Eastern Front, the German army pushed deep into southern Russia, reaching the outskirts of the city of Stalingrad (now Volgograd) by August 1942. Though the city was soon reduced to rubble, the Russian forces under Marshal Semyon Timoshenko doggedly held on. They turned apartment blocks, factories and office buildings into strongholds bristling with heavily armed defenders, forcing the Germans to fight for every last basement, staircase and sewer; the Germans called it the *Rattenkrieg* ('Rat War').

'The enemy is at the gate.
It is a question of life and death.'

Leningrad Party Committee Head Andrei Zhdanov, referring to the German Army encircling the city of Stalingrad

By the autumn the German 6th Army was exhausted and running low on food and ammunition. When the Soviets counter-attacked, the 6th Army found itself surrounded. Hitler stubbornly refused to allow the German general Friedrich von Paulus to retreat or surrender. The Luftwaffe's efforts to supply the troops on the ground were frustrated by freezing fog and a shortage of planes, many of which had been switched to the North African campaign.

When a German attempt to create a corridor for supplies failed, von Paulus's army was doomed. Over 1,300 German soldiers died from frostbite on Christmas Day alone. Von Paulus, ignoring Hitler's order to commit suicide, surrendered on 31 January 1943.

Though the whole of Stalingrad had been flattened, the German surrender marked the first major defeat of Hitler's armies. It had taken over three years. In the meantime, civilians all over Europe were experiencing the true meaning of 'Total War'.

Death by any other name

During the Battle of Stalingrad the Germans used a gigantic 800 mm railway gun, nicknamed 'Dora'. It was one of many weapons to get its own moniker:

- German troops coined the term 'Stalin's organ pipes' for the Russian Katyushka rockets, due to the whooshing sound they made as they were launched.

- German V-1 rockets were called 'buzz bombs' because of their distinctive sound. This may also be the origin of the weapon's other nickname, 'doodlebug' – a buzzing dragonfly.

- The V-2 Rockets were known as 'Bob Hopes', after the popular American comedian. Supposedly the only thing to do if you heard one coming was to 'bob down and hope for the best'!

- No-one is quite sure how the Jeep got its name, but let's go with the story that it came from Eugene the Jeep, a magical character in the *Popeye* comic strip who could do almost anything.

- The bazooka, a rocket launcher that could be fired from the shoulder like a rifle, got its name from a humorous trumpet-like instrument invented and played by US comedian Bob Burns in the 1930s.

- German troops called Sherman tanks 'Tommy cookers', as they often burst into flames after they were hit.

- The howling noise of the missiles fired by the German *Nebelwerfer* rocket launcher led to US soldiers in Sicily giving it the nickname 'Screaming Meemie'.

- Quick-firing British anti-aircraft guns were nicknamed 'Chicago pianos' by US sailors.

- German civilians called air-raid sirens 'Meyer's hunting horn', after Hermann Goering's boast that if a bomb ever fell on the Third Reich, his name would be Meyer (a stereotypical Jewish surname).

- US submarines were known as 'pigboats', as early versions had no periscopes, so attacks were carried out with a bobbing motion like a porpoise, or 'sea pig'.

- The German MG42 machine gun's distinctive ripping sound led to the nickname 'Hitler's zipper'.

- The German S-mine was called a 'Bouncing Betty'. When a victim stepped on it, it sprang into the air before exploding, resulting in a lethal spray of steel balls and metal fragments.

' We'd forgotten
the English fought best with
their backs to the wall. '

Hermann Goering, head of the German air
force, during the Battle of Britain

CHAPTER THREE

NATIONS AT WAR

H itler's generals won a string of brilliant victories in the early years of the war. Even so, the Führer must have known that Germany could never sustain a long war against both America and Russia. Both sides were stretched to the limit, and when push came to shove the war was won on the factory floor as much as on the battlefield.

The Soviets understood this as well as anyone. Having shipped 1,500 entire factories across the Urals, beyond the reach of German tanks and bombers, they employed 6 million workers, mainly women, to crank out guns, shells and battle-winning T-34 tanks. They were producing some 26,000 T-34s annually by 1943, and no less than 40,000 aircraft a year by 1944.

Hitler used slave labour instead, as he wanted German women to stay at home and raise good Nazi families. By 1943, one in five factory workers in Germany (some 12 million people) had been abducted from countries conquered by Germany, especially from Eastern Europe.

Both Britain and the Soviet Union relied heavily on US weapons and supplies. Military spending in America jumped from $1.9 billion in 1940 to $59.8 billion in 1945. The results were impressive:

- Shipbuilding increased by 600 per cent.
- By 1944, a new plane was built every five minutes.
- Over 2.3 million trucks were built by the end of the war.

Atrocities

The chaos of war brings out the worst as well as the best in human nature.

- **The Holocaust** (also known as **Shoah**, Hebrew for 'calamity'). The Germans and their allies systematically murdered between 11 million and 17 million people, including Jews, Gypsies (Romani), Soviet POWs, Polish and Russian civilians, gays, and people with disabilities (see further pages 133–139).

- **Massacres.** Starting in December 1937, over six weeks Japanese soldiers slaughtered at least 150,000 Chinese people in the city of Nanking. Victims were beheaded, burned, bayonetted or buried alive.

  When the Germans crushed the uprising by the Jews in the Warsaw Ghetto, over 55,000 civilians were either killed on the spot or deported to concentration camps.

  Other towns annihilated by the Germans include Kalavryta in Greece, where 1,200 civilians died; Oradour-sur-Glane in France, where 642 men, women and children were killed; and Vinkt in Belgium, where at least 86 civilians were massacred.

- **Starvation.** During the war over 2 million people starved to death in Russia, 3 million in Bengal, 1–2 million in Vietnam and perhaps 3 million in China.

- **Rape.** The Red Army raped an estimated 2 million German women aged between 13 and 70.

- **Medical experiments.** In 2011 Japan began its first formal investigation into the notorious Unit 731, which used prisoners as medical guinea-pigs to research germ warfare and the effects of injuries. The victims, mainly Chinese, may number over 200,000.

  Dr Josef Mengele (the so-called 'Angel of Death') used about 3,000 twins, mostly Romani and Jewish children, for genetic experiments. Only about 200 survived.

- **War trophies.** It is said that US president Franklin Roosevelt received a gift of a letter-opener made from a Japanese man's arm; he ordered it to be decently buried.

- **Cannibalism.** There were reports of cannibalism during the siege of Leningrad. In a 1947 war crimes trial, five Japanese soldiers were convicted and hanged for eating captured prisoners.

- **Betrayal.** At the end of the war, the British and other Allies packed at least 45,000 Cossack prisoners (who had fought alongside the Germans) onto trains heading for the Soviet Union. Government documents that became public in the 1970s show that British commanders knew the prisoners would be executed.

Welders, warriors and witches

- In the United States and Britain, women worked in factories and farms or as mechanics and drivers, while others served on the front line as nurses, doctors and radio operators.

- The American poster girl 'Rosie the Riveter' was supposedly based on Rosina B. Bonavita, who with a colleague fixed 3,345 rivets on an aircraft wing in just six hours. Ignore the glamour shots done for propaganda – this was incredibly hard work and 200 women a day were injured on the job.

- In Germany some 3,700 women served as guards in Nazi concentration camps. One of the most notorious, Ilse Koch, known as 'The Witch of Buchenwald', was later accused of making souvenirs from the skin of murdered inmates with distinctive tattoos.

- In Poland, several thousand women fought in the Resistance during the Warsaw Rising of 1944. One of them, Wanda Gertz, who led the DYSK (women's sabotage unit), was later given two of Poland's highest awards.

- Many women were used as secret agents by the Allies. Among the most famous were the French-born Violette Szabo and Odette Churchill, who were both captured and tortured, and the American Virginia Hall, who was top of the Nazi most-wanted list after masterminding many raids by French Resistance fighters. This queen of disguises learned how to walk without a limp despite having a wooden leg, and once dressed as a milkmaid to evade capture.

- While British and US women pilots delivered newly built planes to airfields, the Soviet Union formed three regiments of women combat pilots to carry out night bombing raids over Germany; they were known to the Germans as 'Night Witches'. By the end of the war, one in ten Russian pilots was female; some, such as Lydia 'Lilya' Litvyak and Katya Budanova, became celebrated fighter aces.

- A million women served in the Red Army as machine gunners, tank crew members and snipers. One female sniper, Lyudmila Pavlichenko, had 309 confirmed kills, including 36 enemy snipers. But very few women were ever promoted to officers.

Russian 'Night Witches'

The American equipment was very welcome, but the tricky part was shipping it past the 'wolf packs' of German submarines waiting in ambush in the grey, stormy seas of the Atlantic Ocean. If the Allies had lost the Battle for the Atlantic, as this naval war was known, they probably would have lost the entire war.

Allied merchant ships sailed in large groups known as convoys, protected by small warships. Even so, in the early part of the war German submarines, or U-boats, inflicted enormous damage using deck guns or torpedoes. Countless seamen died terrible deaths, burnt in flaming ships, choking on oil or drowning in the Atlantic. Often whole crews went down with the ship. When the United States joined the war, things initially got worse: from January to August 1942, known as the 'American shooting season' by U-boat commanders, the Germans sank 609 ships for the loss of only 22 U-boats.

Britain came dangerously close to running out of supplies, until its codebreakers cracked secret German naval codes so the Allies could intercept orders to the U-boats. Improved

115

radar forced the U-boats to attack from underwater, while new long-range aircraft attacked them with depth charges from bases in Iceland. As a result, by the end of the war two out of three U-boats had been sunk and 30,000 German submariners had been killed. The Allied supremacy at sea was such that when 2 million soldiers were shipped across the Channel in June 1944 in the build-up to D-Day, there were remarkably few losses.

The Home front

In World War Two, no-one was safe. Mercifully, gas was never used in bombing raids, but high explosives and incendiary bombs brought their own horrors. In Britain, as in Germany and Japan later in the war, children were evacuated from cities as a precaution.

The Blitz was terrifying enough, but there was a very real fear in 1940–41 that the English countryside would soon be crawling with German tanks while parachutists dropped from the sky in their thousands. By June 1940, 1,500,000 men ineligible for military

service had joined the Home Guard, from boys as young as 14 to 80-year-olds, though the majority were in their forties or fifties, many with battle experience from the First World War.

At first this 'Dad's Army' (as it is now affectionately called) was armed with an assortment of pikes, catapults, shotguns, pitchforks and golf clubs. Though by 1942 they were properly armed and trained, they probably wouldn't have troubled a crack German panzer regiment for long.

In the event, the closest the Home Guard came to seeing action was on 7 September 1940, when the signal for an imminent invasion went out after a false report of a paratrooper led to some church bells being rung in alarm.

The Home Guard's original name, Local Defence Volunteers, was dropped after the members had to put up with disparaging jokes such as 'Long-Dentured Veterans' and 'Look–Duck–Vanish.'

Dad's Army

The Home Guard did valuable work clearing rubble, guarding damaged banks, acting as sentries and patrolling the countryside. But it was often hampered by lack of training and poor equipment:

- One platoon in Staffordshire chose their commander simply by asking: 'Any man here with Army experience and who has a car?'

- A recommended method for unmasking German spies was to shout 'Heil Hitler!', in the belief that they wouldn't be able to stop themselves saluting back.

- Some 50 or so Home Guards were shot by their own men, due to jumpy guards mistaking them for the enemy.

- The badly designed 'sticky bombs' – anti-tank grenades shaped like thermos flasks – killed almost 80 Home Guard members and injured many more as the sticks came loose and the bombs fell at their feet.

- Almost anyone parachuting out of the sky was assumed to be the enemy, so RAF pilots who had been shot down were sometimes attacked by the Home Guard.

While Australia suffered Japanese air raids and invasion scares, life in Canada and the United States carried on much as normal, though people generally worked much longer hours and meat, petrol and clothing were rationed. To help the war effort, most ordinary Americans did their bit by buying war bonds, collecting scrap aluminium and cooking grease, and planting 'victory gardens' to grow their own fruit and veg.

Though the Axis forces never had any serious plans to invade America, the Nazis hoped to create havoc there by sabotaging factories, canals and railways. But Operation Pastorius, launched in June 1942, was a disaster. The team leader defected and turned himself in to the FBI. Within two weeks all the other seven members were arrested and six were later executed. The Americans were more worried about U-boat attacks in US waters. President Roosevelt came up with the idea of 'Hooligan's Navy', a fleet of amateur sailors (among them the novelist Ernest Hemingway), to patrol the nation's shores. But the large number of false sightings was not a good use of the US Navy's time.

Behind barbed wire

- In March 1942 the US government, swayed by public hostility after the attack on Pearl Harbor, rounded up some 120,000 Japanese Americans, many of them children, and put them into camps ringed by armed soldiers and barbed wire for the rest of the war.

- In Britain, thousands of Germans, Austrians and Italians were interned, many on the Isle of Man. Another 7,000 were deported to Canada and Australia. But an outcry over their poor treatment meant that many were released by the summer of 1941.

- In America, over 400,000 Italian and German POWs were allowed out of camps to work as farm labourers, loggers and cannery workers. Some stayed, and married local women.

- Most British and American POWs did not suffer too badly at the hands of their German captors. But, out of the 5.7 million Russians captured, 3.5 million had died in German camps by the end of the war.

- One in four Allied POWs died in Japanese captivity. From all over Asia came reports of prisoners turned to skeletons by starvation, of men worked to death in their thousands or beheaded for small acts of disobedience. The Japanese believed soldiers should die rather than allow themselves to be captured.

Stalin and the Soviet Union were definitely caught napping when the Germans attacked in 1941, and by 1942 half the Russian population had been conquered. Soviet farms were desperately short of workers, tools and equipment, and food production plummeted. While in the cities factory workers received rations, most fed themselves from small private plots.

The Soviet people were caught between the devil and the deep blue sea, with the Germans wiping them out in the thousands while Stalin deported a million Soviet citizens to Siberia and locked up another 1.5 million in the GULAG prison camps. Here they were slave labourers working in mines or arms factories or building railways. Amazingly, Soviet morale remained high, and belief in Mother Russia was strong.

Life for many Germans was fairly comfortable in the early years of the war, as the Nazis plundered conquered lands. Morale held firm until 1942, but as the tide turned, goods became scarce and German cities suffered heavy bombing. There was no large-scale

resistance to the Nazis, though small groups of military and civilian conspirators hatched several plots to kill or depose Hitler; a number of German aristocrats volunteered for suicide attacks. Other Germans helped victims of the regime by providing food, false documents and safe-houses.

The war was unpopular in Italy, and many Italians had little faith in Mussolini, dubbed the 'sawdust Caesar' by US journalist George Seldes. Though the black market thrived in Italy, there were often shortages of food. The rise in Allied bombing raids from 1942 led to a stream of refugees into the countryside from big cities such as Milan.

After the fall of Mussolini, Italy descended into civil war, fought between fascist groups such as the Brigate Nere (Black Brigades) and partisan groups that formed in the mountains. The Germans treated their former allies like any other conquered nation, shooting civilians in revenge for partisan activities and sending Italian soldiers to work in German factories.

Totally bunkers?

In October 1940 Hitler ordered the construction of bomb shelters and flak towers (tall concrete blockhouses fitted with anti-aircraft guns) in all the major cities, in a programme that employed some 80,000 workers. Whereas London's underground air-raid shelters aimed to protect just 1 per cent of people at risk, in Germany this figure was nearer 5 per cent. After the war these structures proved to be very hard to demolish, and for many of them new uses were found:

- Some became accommodation for students.

- In Hamburg, a huge bunker became the city's first television centre.

- A converted bunker in Berlin is home to the Boros Collection of modern art.

- In Frankfurt, a bunker was turned into musicians' studios.

- German bunkers are not the only ones that have been given a new lease of life: a bunker in Cornwall, England, has recently been turned into a four-bedroom bungalow, while a bomb shelter in Stockholm now houses two of the WikiLeaks servers.

The Japanese home front was not well organised. As in Germany, women expected to stay at home rather than work in factories. Out of an age-old tradition of duty, many Japanese accepted the hardships of war. When large-scale US bombing began in 1944, some 10 million people fled from the cities to the countryside. The Japanese equivalent of the Home Guard, the People's Volunteer Combat Corps, was trained to resist the invader with bamboo pikes.

Life in neutral countries was something of a balancing act. Over 10,000 Portuguese fought for Britain in northern France due to a long-standing alliance, and the Swedes secretly sent troops to fight against Germany.

In Ireland, the Second World War was known as 'the Emergency'. Documents found after the war showed that Hitler planned to use Ireland as a springboard to attack Britain: the plan was codenamed Operation Green. But the invasion had to be called off after the German army got bogged down in Russia.

Wabbit Stew

Most people these days don't have the stomach for squirrel-tail soup or crow pie, two of the more extreme recipes promoted by the British government as part of its campaign to make rations last longer.

But the authorities also encouraged people to keep rabbits and grow their own vegetables in gardens and allotments. French farmers also kept rabbits so they could swap them for bread and cigarettes on the black market. With all this in mind, here is a recipe for a tasty rabbit stew. Be thankful your meal won't be disturbed by the sound of approaching bombers.

Ingredients:

- 1 whole rabbit, cut into stew-sized pieces
- 1 tbsp vinegar
- 1 oz (25 g) plain flour
- a pinch of salt and freshly ground pepper
- 1–2 oz lard or dripping
- 2 bacon rashers, with rinds if possible
- 2 medium onions, sliced
- 3 medium carrots, sliced
- 4 medium potatoes, diced
- 1 pint (600 ml) water or stock
- 1 cooking apple
- fresh herbs, e.g. parsley or bay leaves

Method:

1. Steep the rabbit in a mix of cold water and vinegar for about an hour.

2. Strain off the liquid, then pat the rabbit pieces dry.

3. Coat the meat with flour. Season with salt and pepper.

4. Cut the rind from the bacon and add it to the lard in a pot.

5. On a medium heat, fry the rabbit meat for about 10 minutes, until it browns.

6. Peel, core and grate the apple and chop the potatoes, carrots, onions and bacon. Then gently cook them in the pot for about 5 minutes.

7. Add the stock and herbs to the pot, if you are using them, and bring to the boil, stirring to thicken.

8. Turn the heat down and simmer for 30 minutes.

The Irish government started its own shipping firm to bring in supplies, but food was still scarce and ration books were needed to buy butter, tea and bread. Inspectors known as 'glimmermen' cut off the gas if anyone used too much.

In Northern Ireland (part of the United Kingdom), farms and businesses supplied goods for the war, and its ports were used by British ships. In 1941 German planes bombed the capital, Belfast, killing over 1,000 people.

Truth: the first casualty of war

Governments on both sides were happy to tell lies to gain support and boost morale, using posters, radio and cinema newsreels. 'Tokyo Rose' (the US-born Iva Ikuko Toguri) spoke to US soldiers, and Irish-American fascist William Joyce, nicknamed Lord Haw-Haw, broadcast to Britain for the Nazis. In 1940, up to 18 million listeners were tuning in to his programmes – many felt they didn't get the whole truth from the BBC.

Propaganda messages

- Keep calm and carry on. (Britain)

- Dig for victory. (Britain)

- Be like Dad: keep Mum. (Britain)

- Careless talk costs lives. (Britain)

- When you ride alone you ride with Hitler; join a car-sharing club today. (United States)

- One battle, one will, one goal: victory at any cost! (Germany)

- Shame on you, chatterer! The enemy is listening. Silence is your duty. (Germany)

- Farmer! You are a soldier in the battle of production. (Germany)

- Fire and Never Quit! (Japan)

- You're damned. Go to the devil! (Japanese leaflet dropped on US troops)

And here's some health and safety advice for US servicemen tempted by foreign seductresses:

- She may be a bag of trouble: syphilis, gonorrhea.

US and American propaganda did their best to make Hitler look like a buffoon – though this had little effect in Germany, where propaganda chief Joseph Goebbels managed to inspire trust in the Führer almost to the end of the war. Leaflets were also dropped on enemy lines to encourage troops to desert or surrender.

Many countries produced propaganda films, and while films such as *Casablanca*, *The Great Dictator* and *In Which We Serve* are rightly famous, some of the most effective were made by Japan. The remarkable 1945 French film, *Les Enfants du Paradis*, was made during the German occupation of France. Many of the 1,800 extras were Resistance agents using the film as daytime cover!

Singing stars such as Vera Lynn and Dinah Shore, comedians Bob Hope and George Formby, and band leader Glenn Miller toured hospitals and factories and performed for troops behind the front lines. The Soviet Union had over 1,000 touring companies. On occasion, soldiers went off to fight then returned to watch the rest of the show.

famous wartime songs

German
- Lili Marlene (perhaps the most popular song of World War Two with both German and British forces)
- Berlin is Still Berlin

American
- (There'll Be Bluebirds Over) The White Cliffs of Dover
- Boogie Woogie Bugle Boy
- Coming in on a Wing and a Prayer

British
- We'll Meet Again
- Knees Up, Mother Brown
- Roll Out the Barrel
- Blackout Stroll
- Run, Rabbit, Run
- There'll Always Be an England

Russian
- Katyusha (about a girl longing for her beloved, who is away on military service)
- Farewell of Slavianka (a patriotic march)
- *Svyashchennaya Voyna* (The Sacred War)

Australian
- We're Off To See the Wizard (from *The Wizard of Oz* – a marching song popular with Australian troops)

Living with the enemy

Thanks to the Gestapo and its network of informers, most of occupied Europe lived in a constant state of fear. Russians were forced to wear numbers on their clothes, and hundreds of thousands of East Europeans were transported to Germany and forced to work 18-hour days manufacturing arms for the German forces.

Many co-operated with the Nazis: by the end of the war, some 300,000 non-Germans had joined the SS. In France, local men joined a paramilitary police force, the Milice. But others fought back by carrying out raids on German bases or convoys, stealing secrets, or helping shot-down pilots, POWs on the run, or escaping Jews.

Across Asia, local peoples were forced to bow to Japanese soldiers and to learn Japanese in schools. Both Germans and Japanese plundered the resources of conquered nations, from food and raw materials to luxury goods and works of art.

The spoils of war

During the invasion and occupation of Europe, leading Nazis hoarded vast amounts of art and gold, and any other valuables they could lay their hands on.

- Each country had secret hiding places for its treasures. In France, works including Leonardo da Vinci's *Mona Lisa* and the statue known as the *Venus de Milo* were stored in châteaux in the south and west of the country. Britain evacuated many of its cultural treasures to quarries in Wales or to museums in the United States and Canada. In the Netherlands, museums hid objects in barges and bunkers.

- Many of these hideouts didn't stay secret for long. In Warsaw alone, a total of 13,512 paintings and 1,379 sculptures were stolen.

- Many myths have grown up over the missing treasures. In 2011 British treasure hunters started searching the Stolpsee, a lake near Berlin, for 18 boxes of gold apparently thrown into its depths by Polish slave workers as the Red Army approached. Another legend tells how the crew of a U-boat buried a fortune in gold on uninhabited Auckland Island, which lies a few hundred kilometres south of New Zealand.

The Holocaust

Soon after coming to power in 1933, Hitler changed the law in Germany to allow the Nazis to round up their political enemies and place them in 'police detention' – in reality, concentration camps. The first prisoners were communists, political opponents or gypsies, who were forced to do hard physical labour.

The war led to a new kind of camp, built solely to kill large groups of people quickly and efficiently. Hitler had long harboured a special hatred of Jews. The Nazis believed that Germans were 'racially superior' and that the Jews were a threat to Germany. From the outset of the war, SS Einsatzgruppen (murder squads) hunted down Jews and executed them, often with the help of local people. By the end of 1941 a million Jews had been killed – mostly shot, then buried in mass graves.

Jewish families were forced out of their homes and moved into designated areas known as ghettos (from the name of the medieval Jewish quarter in Venice). There were major ghettos in Białystok, Kovno, Łódź, Minsk,

Riga and Vilnius, but the largest was in the Polish capital Warsaw, with a population of 445,000 by March 1941. In November 1940 the Warsaw ghetto was walled in and became effectively a prison.

But this was merely a preparation for the final, nightmarish phase of Hitler's genocidal plan. On 20 January 1942 the Nazis decided on the 'Final Solution': the systematic destruction of all Jews by gassing them to death.

> 'The Führer has ordered that the Jewish question be settled once and for all... Every Jew that we lay our hands on has to be destroyed.'
>
> *Heinrich Himmler, summer 1941*

The operation was masterminded by SS General Reinhard Heydrich and Adolf Eichmann, head of the Gestapo Jewish Affairs section. The six main death camps were constructed in Poland, the country with the largest Jewish population. From all over Europe, Jews were brought to the camps by train. Many died on the journey from starvation, thirst or disease.

'Re-education'

The Nazis did their best to hide their deadly secret from the outside world, referring to the death camps by misleading names such as 're-education camps'. Prisoners at Theresienstadt concentration camp were forced to make a propaganda film entitled *Hitler Presents a Town to the Jews*. They so obviously exaggerated the kindness of the Nazi guards that the film was never released. As punishment, many were sent to their deaths at Auschwitz.

Operation Bernhard

SS officer Bernhard Krüger set up a team of 142 counterfeiters using inmates at Sachsenhausen and other concentration camps, creating the largest counterfeiting operation in history. The Nazis hoped to destabilise the British economy by flooding the country with forged notes. But the Bank of England had been tipped off and soon spotted the forgeries.

At the end of the war, large bundles of fake pounds ended up in the hands of the Jewish underground, who used them to buy equipment and to bring refugees to Palestine.

Holocaust heroes

- **Anne Frank** was an ordinary Jewish girl who was forced to go into hiding after the Nazis invaded the Netherlands. She and her family, along with four others, spent 25 months in a set of rooms above her father's office in Amsterdam. After their hiding place was betrayed to the Nazis, the family was arrested and deported to Nazi concentration camps in Poland. In March 1945 Anne died of typhus at Bergen-Belsen camp, aged 15. Her diary, saved by one of the family's helpers, Miep Gies, was published in 1947. Today it is one of the most widely read books in the world.

- **Oskar Schindler** was an unlikely hero – a Nazi who initially hoped to profit from the war by employing Jewish slave labourers at his enamelware factory in Poland. Appalled by Nazi brutality, he began smuggling children out of ghettos and moved hundreds of Jewish women and children from the camps to his factory, claiming that their skills were vital to his business. He is buried in Jerusalem – a unique honour for a Nazi Party member.

- As soon as Swedish diplomat **Raoul Wallenberg** arrived at the Swedish embassy in Budapest in July 1944, he began issuing Swedish passports to thousands of Jews, preventing their deportation to death camps. He rented buildings to house Jewish refugees, declaring them to be Swedish diplomatic territory. Having saved possibly 100,000 Jews, he was captured by Red Army troops and died in a Soviet prison in 1947.

- **Irena Sendler** smuggled some 2,500 children out of the Warsaw ghetto and had them placed in Polish families, orphanages and convents. Arrested, tortured and sentenced to death by the Gestapo in 1943, she was rescued and in 2003 was awarded Poland's highest civilian decoration, the Order of the White Eagle.

- In Prague in 1939, British stockbroker **Nicholas Winton** saved 669 children from the death camps by finding them foster parents in England and Sweden. His exploits became known only in 1988 when his wife discovered lists of the children and letters from their parents.

- **Chiune Sugihara.** A diplomat working in the Japanese consulate in Kaunas, Lithuania, in 1939, Sugihara deliberately broke the rules and issued exit visas to Polish and Lithuanian Jews. Mobbed by desperate refugees as he boarded a train out of the country, he was unable to stamp all their visas so threw the official stamp to the crowd, saving perhaps as many as 10,000 Jews.

- In 1943 the **Danish Resistance**, helped by many ordinary Danish citizens, evacuated over 7,500 Danish Jews to neutral Sweden. Some were transported in large fishing boats, others in rowing boats or kayaks.

The camps were guarded by members of the brutal SS 'Death's-Head' units. Prisoners had identification numbers tattooed on their arms, and the standard clothing was a striped uniform with a patch for different categories of prisoner: yellow for Jews, green for criminals and red for political prisoners.

In some camps, such as Treblinka, all prisoners were killed on arrival. They were told to undress for a shower, then herded into specially built chambers where they were killed by poison gas poured through the ceiling. The bodies were burnt in giant incinerators. In other camps, including Auschwitz, some prisoners were worked to death instead.

Stories of what was happening filtered across Europe, a grim warning to anyone who stood up to the Nazis. A rebellion in the Warsaw ghetto held out for 28 days but stood little chance against German forces armed with tanks. In Sobibór camp, where 250,000 Jews were murdered, there was a mass breakout of 600 prisoners in October 1943. SS guards were lured to their deaths in storerooms.

Within an hour, the camp was burning and the first group of prisoners fled across the surrounding minefields. Though 300 of them eventually got away, just 50 survived the war.

In the final months of the war, SS guards moved camp inmates by train or on forced marches, often called 'death marches', to prevent the Allies freeing them. The Nazis were so determined to carry out the Final Solution that the marches continued until 7 May 1945, the day the German armed forces finally surrendered to the Allies.

The deliberate and systematic murder of millions of people by the Nazis, generally known as the Holocaust (from a Greek word for 'sacrifice'), is more horrible than most people can imagine. Yet, despite the overwhelming evidence of the crimes carried out by the Nazis, some people today attempt to deny that it ever happened. At a time when the remaining survivors of the camps are reaching the end of their lives, these shocking events should not be forgotten.

The children's war

Many children had to cope with evacuation, the loss of a relative, or the threat of invasion. Others experienced the vicissitudes of war first-hand.

- **Rejected.** Some 200,000 children, cruelly nicknamed 'Boche babies', were the result of liaisons between German soldiers and French women during the war. Only 60 years later were they awarded German citizenship. Children were born in similar circumstances across occupied Europe and Asia.

- **Trained.** British and German children were taught air-raid drills, how to build air-raid shelters, how to use gas masks, and how to fight fires. Soviet children were expected to know how to take care of wounded soldiers and how to defend themselves against enemy attack.

- **Evacuated.** In Britain, evacuees were usually placed with host families in rural areas. In 1941, 264,000 Russian children were evacuated from Leningrad alone, while 70,000 German children were sent to occupied Denmark, where many died.

- **Taught in secret.** The Germans destroyed or closed many schools in Russia. To counter this, partisans often tried to provide secret networks to teach local children.

- **Enlisted.** Orphans adopted by Soviet regiments lived and fought alongside them. The Germans manned an entire SS tank division with 16- and 17-year-old boys from the Hitler Youth. A 15-year-old Yugoslavian boy, Boško Buha, formed a battalion of teenage grenade-throwers. Fearing invasion in 1945, the Japanese trained teenagers to fight with bamboo spears. Many Jewish teenagers fought in the Jewish Resistance.

- **Kidnapped.** Polish children with blond hair and 'Aryan' looks were taken away and brought up in Germany.

- **Orphaned.** At the end of the war, thousands of orphaned children were in displaced-persons camps. Many surviving Jewish children fled from Eastern Europe as part of the mass exodus (*Brihah* or *Bricha*) to the western zones of occupied Germany, en route to Palestine and later Israel.

- **Killed.** The Germans and their collaborators killed as many as 1.5 million children, including over a million Jewish children and tens of thousands of Romani (Gypsy) children and German children with physical and mental disabilities.

- **Saved.** From 1938 to 1940 the rescue effort known as the *Kindertransport* (Children's Transport) brought thousands of Jewish children (without their parents) to safety in Great Britain and Ireland.

'Sure, we want to go home. We want this war over with. The quickest way to get it over with is to go get the bastards who started it. '

US General George S. Patton, addressing his troops before D-Day

CHAPTER FOUR

THE LONG FIGHT BACK

Stalingrad was a major blow to Hitler's plans. But in the spring of 1943 a bulge in the Soviet line around the city of Kursk, some 800 km south of Moscow, gave the Germans a chance to encircle and destroy three Soviet army groups. It was a high-risk strategy, but Hitler's generals had two new toys to play with: the powerful Panther and Tiger tanks, which they believed would be more than a match for the Soviet T-34. (In battle, however, the Panther and Tiger proved rather unreliable beasts.)

'Whenever I think of this attack,
my stomach churns.'

Hitler, prior to the Battle of Kursk

On 5 July the Germans attacked with a force of 2,700 tanks and assault guns, 1,800 aircraft and some 900,000 men – kicking off the biggest battle in history. But, thanks to their Lucy spy ring in Switzerland, the Soviets had prepared their response. They massed huge numbers of artillery and rocket launchers behind defences reinforced with 400,000 mines and 5,000 km of trenches.

A whiff of trouble

Soviet soldiers were apparently rather good at hiding in trees or long grass, waiting in silence while the enemy marched past, oblivious to their presence. To counter this, German patrols were led by non-smokers – they were more likely to smell the enemy's tobacco and sweat, or the cheap perfume they used to ward off lice.

The battle raged for eight days, much of it in the pouring rain. Though the Germans destroyed some 2,300 tanks to 400 of their own, they failed to break through. After Kursk, the Soviets, now churning out tanks in ever-growing numbers, were more powerful than the Germans and their allies on the Eastern Front. The long retreat back to Berlin had begun.

Meanwhile, the offensive in Russia had been seriously undermined by the Allied invasion of Sicily on 10 July 1943, forcing the Germans to switch forces to Italy. The defeat of the Afrika Korps in May 1943 had allowed the Allies to use Tunisia as a springboard to attack Sicily, which they captured in five weeks.

By now, Mussolini had been put in prison by the Italian government, and on 3 September the Italians surrendered; the Allies crossed into mainland Italy on the same day. After a US force landed at Salerno, many Italians changed sides. Others were disarmed by the Germans, who invaded northern Italy. On Cephalonia, 5,000 Italians who resisted the Germans were executed for 'treason'.

Operation Mincemeat

One April morning in 1943, a sardine fisherman spotted the corpse of a British officer, Major William Martin, floating in the sea off the coast of Spain. Back on shore, German agents soon heard about the discovery and learned that the dead body was carrying top-secret papers that revealed an Allied plan to invade Sardinia. 'Major Martin' was in fact a victim of pneumonia, and the papers in the briefcase chained to his wrist had been faked by Royal Naval Intelligence. The ruse (dramatised in the novel and film *The Man Who Never Was*) saved thousands of lives by sending German troops in the wrong direction.

In early July 1943 the RAF had hatched a bold plan to assassinate Mussolini at his headquarters in Rome with a rooftop bombing raid by the 'Dambusters' squadron. The attack never took place, but the Germans showed how it could be done when a daring rescue led by Otto Skorzeny snatched Mussolini from his mountain-top prison. The Duce formed a new government, but by now he was little more than a German puppet.

On the Eastern Front, despite Russian successes, Stalin demanded more support from the Allies. They copied the Blitz tactics, attacking German cities in huge daylight air raids using heavily armoured B-17 Flying Fortress and B-24 Liberator bombers.

On 30 May 1942 the first 1,000-bomber raid on the city of Cologne was ordered by Air Vice Marshal Arthur 'Bomber' Harris. Crews were highly vulnerable to enemy fighter planes and flak – by the end of the war, 8,000 bombers and 40,000 aircrew had been lost. Some relief came with the arrival of long-range fighter escorts such as the P-51 Mustang, while 'pathfinder' squadrons of Mosquito fighter-bombers with electronic bombing aids greatly improved bombing accuracy.

By the end of the war the Allies had dropped 3.4 million tonnes of bombs. Strategically the raids were a success, diverting artillery, ammunition and planes badly needed elsewhere. But they were hell on earth for the civilian population: high-explosive bombs were followed by incendiary bombs, creating violent winds that sucked people into the flames.

Island hoppers

In the Pacific, the Allies battled to win back territory conquered by the Japanese in the early part of the war. General Douglas MacArthur, true to his word, led an offensive though New Guinea and the Philippines, while Admiral Chester Nimitz island-hopped across the Pacific towards Japan.

The US assault on Guadalcanal in the Solomon Islands, beginning in August 1942, typified the war in the Pacific. For six months, savage battles were fought on sandy beaches and in dense jungles in an attempt to control Henderson Field, the large airstrip on the island. The Japanese were eventually overwhelmed by the sheer weight of American numbers. When defeat looked certain, many died where they stood rather than surrender.

Guadalcanal was America's Kursk in the Pacific, and from now on Japanese forces were on the retreat. In Burma, British and Indian troops, known as Chindits, began a guerrilla campaign deep behind enemy lines. Though they suffered heavy casualties,

the campaign provided a much-needed propaganda boost back home.

In June 1944 US forces attacked the Marianas Islands, part of Japan's defensive ring. During the battle, a Japanese fleet with four aircraft carriers counter-attacked. But the Japanese Mitsubishi Type 0 fighters, known to the Allies as 'Zeros', were no match for the latest US planes. On 19 June, 219 Japanese planes were shot down for the loss of just 29 US planes. On the same day, US submarines and planes sank three Japanese aircraft carriers, marking the end of Japan's naval air power.

By August 1944 US forces were on a roll, having taken the islands of Saipan, Tinian and Guam in the Marianas. The airfields here would allow US B-29 Superfortress bombers to attack Japan's cities 2,000 km to the north. Two months later a large US invasion force headed for Leyte in the Philippines, destroying 26 Japanese ships.

Desperate measures

The more desperate things got, the harder the Japanese fought. Kamikaze pilots deliberately steered their planes into US ships, sinking 34 ships and damaging over 280 others in just 12 months. (*Kamikaze* means 'Divine Wind' in Japanese, referring to a storm in 1281 that destroyed a Mongol invasion fleet.) Some Japanese commanders objected to the waste of pilots' lives; others felt there was no alternative.

But kamikaze pilots weren't the only ones willing to sacrifice all for their country:

- Japanese suicide torpedo craft, known as *Kaiten* ('Heaven Shakers'), were less successful, sinking just one ship.

- When defeat was imminent, Japanese infantry carried out mass attacks shouting *Tenno heika banzai* ('Long live the Emperor') as they advanced.

- Using V-1 flying bombs fitted with a cockpit, the Nazis believed that 1,000 suicide pilots could effectively wipe out an Allied invasion fleet. But D-Day came and went before the project was fully developed.

- Towards the end of the war, the Luftwaffe did resort to missions that were almost suicidal. On a daylight raid on 7 April 1945, 20 US bombers were deliberately rammed by German fighters from the Sonderkommando Elbe unit. Pilots were expected to parachute out of their planes at the last moment, but without ejector seats this was rarely successful.

- In 1942 Joseph Stalin decreed that no Soviet soldier was allowed to retreat or get captured. Anyone who did (and later got liberated) was sent to one of the penal battalions. These units were first in line for suicide missions. 'Tramplers', for example, ran ahead of advancing troops to trip any mines that might be in their path.

- The Russians trained anti-tank dogs to carry explosives towards enemy tanks. In battle, however, they often ran away – or rushed towards the Soviet tanks they had been trained on.

- Somebody in US military intelligence came up with the mad idea that if you attached a cat to a bomb and dropped it near an enemy ship, the cat would instinctively guide the bomb towards the deck, since (a) cats hate water and (b) they always land on their feet. In practice, the poor moggies tended to pass out mid-drop.

- The US Navy also experimented with a plan to strap incendiary devices to bats and release them over enemy territory. In theory, the bats would then fly into the attics of buildings and set fire to them.

D~Day and beyond

The Allied advance in Italy continued, with landings at Anzio in central Italy on 22 January 1944. It was tough going and gave the Allies a good idea of what to expect if they ever invaded northern France. The key to the German defensive position was the town of Monte Cassino. Though Allied bombers flattened its medieval monastery, the Germans were well dug in. Despite several bloody attacks, some 100,000 Allied troops found themselves penned in on a narrow strip of land.

There was a lull for several weeks, during which time the Allied troops amused themselves by betting on horse races along the beach, or on beetles painted in racing colours. They set up makeshift stills brewing a potent concoction known as Kickapoo Joy Juice. It's said that one drunk GI blundered into German lines wearing a top hat. Amazingly, the Germans simply turned him around and sent him back to his own lines.

In May 1944 the Allies finally broke through at Monte Cassino. US soldiers entered Rome

on 4 June, only to have their thunder stolen by the D-Day landings two days later. By the end of the war, only a small part of northern Italy was in German hands. In April 1945 Mussolini was captured and executed by Italian partisans, along with his mistress Clara Petacci. After being kicked and spat on by an angry mob, their bodies were strung up from the roof of a petrol station in Milan.

The Allies had spent two years umming and ah-ing about an invasion of Western Europe, while on the other side of the English Channel the Germans prepared for the inevitable by building a line of fortresses along the northern French coastline, known as the Atlantic Wall.

US general Dwight D. Eisenhower, or 'Ike' as he was known, gambled on landing along a 100-km stretch of coastline in Normandy. While most troops would hit the beaches in landing craft, others would drop behind enemy lines using gliders or by parachuting in. Sherman tanks were fitted with propellers and airbags to allow them to float ashore, while other tanks had flails to destroy the mines on the beaches, or flamethrowers designed to knock out enemy bunkers. Once the beaches were secured, two huge artificial harbours known as Mulberries would be constructed to offload the men, vehicles and supplies needed to sustain the attack.

The Allies went to enormous lengths to convince the Germans that the attack was going to take place at Calais, some 370 km away. Fake equipment dumps, inflatable tanks and buildings made from wood gave the impression of a non-existent army in Kent, while Operation Moonshine used reflective balloons and some electronic wizardry to make a few small ships look like an invasion fleet on German radar.

On 6 June, D-Day, Operation Overlord was launched. Some 6,500 vessels landed over 150,000 Allied forces on five Normandy beaches, codenamed Utah, Omaha, Gold, Juno and Sword. Behind the lines, the French Resistance – alerted by coded messages broadcast by the BBC, such as *Les carottes sont cuites* ('The carrots are cooked') – sabotaged railway lines and telephone exchanges.

The whispers of war

Both sides encouraged servicemen and civilians not to pass on gossip. Across Britain, posters warned that 'Careless talk costs lives,' while in Germany a poster showed how a 'toilet rumour' whispered at 2.00 p.m. could spread to thousands in a couple of hours. Yet many rumours were spread deliberately:

- During the Blitz, the British Underground Propaganda Committee concocted a variety of *sibs* (from the Latin *sibilare* 'to hiss') to deter a German invasion of England, from a deadly machine gun to a secret weapon that would set the sea on fire over a huge area.

- The old chestnut about carrots helping you see in the dark was made up by British intelligence. Rumours were circulated that RAF pilots were fed carrots, as a cover for the fact that they were using a weapon unknown to the Germans – radar.

- Operation Quicksilver, devised by the aptly named Colonel David Strangeways, spread the lie that the First United States Army Group (FUSAG), a totally non-existent force, was going to land near Calais.

- Operation Periwig was set up by British intelligence to fool the Gestapo into hunting down non-existent resistance groups, and, with a little luck, encourage Germans to form their own real ones.

Though the Americans met fierce resistance at Omaha beach, the landings caught the Germans by surprise and Allied casualties were far lower than predicted. The Germans, still convinced that the main attack would come at Calais, were slow to react, and Allied air superiority allowed rocket-firing Typhoon fighter-bombers to blast German reinforcements from above. General Rommel himself was attacked and wounded by a US fighter plane.

Though 850,000 men and 150,000 vehicles were ashore by the end of June, it took six weeks for the Allies to break out from the beachhead. The narrow lanes and high, thick hedgerows of the Normandy countryside were easy to defend. A German counter-attack at Falaise led to heavy British losses, but by 20 August the Germans were in full retreat. By now the French transport system was a shambles, so the Americans came up with the 'Red Ball Express', in which a convoy of 6,000 trucks used a one-way system to deliver supplies to General George Patton's 3rd Army.

'It must be utterly destroyed ... nothing must
be left standing, no church, no artistic
monument'

Hitler's orders on the fate of Paris

Word got out that the Germans were going to
blow up Paris before the Allies got there, so
Eisenhower decided to bypass the city.
Thankfully the German commander Dietrich
von Cholitz ignored Hitler's command and
agreed to surrender, and on 25 August Allied
troops poured into the city. By 4 September
General Montgomery's tanks had reached
Antwerp in Belgium, and a week later the first
US patrols crossed into Germany.

'Maybe there are 5,000, maybe 10,000 Nazi
bastards in their concrete foxholes before the
Third Army. Now if Ike [General Eisenhower]
stops holding Monty's hand and gives me some
supplies, I'll go through the Siegfried Line
like shit through a goose.'

US general George S. Patton

The Allied forces were too exhausted and
overstretched to launch a full-scale attack on
Germany, so Montgomery came up with a
bold plan, named Operation Market Garden.

On 17 September 1944 thousands of Allied paratroopers landed 150 km behind enemy lines. Their goal was to capture the bridges over the Meuse and Rhine rivers, allowing the Allied tanks to skirt around the Siegfried Line, the defences built to protect Germany against French attack. If it worked, the war would be over by Christmas.

Though two bridges were captured, the northern bridge at Arnhem proved to be 'a bridge too far'. After ten days of bitter fighting, just 2,000 paratroopers escaped out of 10,000. After this brave failure, the Allied advance slowed.

In one last roll of the dice, Hitler decided on a counter-attack through the Ardennes forest, to cut the Allies off from their supply base at Antwerp. On 16 December the Germans advanced, taking advantage of fog, snow and the fact that this part of the line, known as the Ghost Front, was manned by resting combat units or new recruits. German commando units dressed as US troops added to the chaos, and the attack, known as the Battle of the Bulge (because that was what the German lines

looked like on the map), only failed when clear blue skies a week later allowed Allied planes to carve up the German tanks and supply lines.

In Eastern Europe, the Germans defended bravely but could do little to stop the massed ranks of a Soviet army almost twice their size. A Russian offensive on 22 June 1944 drove 400 km west to Warsaw, encouraging 40,000 Poles to rebel and recapture a large part of their city. Despite suffering 350,000 casualties, the Germans counter-attacked, driving the Soviets back and killing 200,000 civilians as they razed Warsaw to the ground.

Are you mad?

During the Battle of the Bulge, General Sepp Dietrich summed up the frustration of many German generals with their increasingly delusional commander-in-chief, Adolf Hitler: 'All Hitler wants me to do is cross a river [the mighty Meuse], capture Brussels and take Antwerp. All this at the worst time of the year, through the Ardennes forest when the snow is waist-deep ... with re-formed divisions made up chiefly of kids and sick old men – and at Christmas.'

Even this did little to slow the Red tide, and by the end of 1944 the Soviets had taken Romania, Estonia and Hungary. As they moved across Europe, Soviet soldiers began to encounter tens of thousands of concentration-camp prisoners. In January 1945 the Soviets liberated Auschwitz. Though the Nazis had forced the majority of prisoners west in what became known as 'death marches', the appalling horrors of the Holocaust were clear to see. At Auschwitz the Russians found over 800,000 women's outfits and more than 7,000 kg of human hair. In the coming months, as more camps were liberated by Soviet, British and US forces, the scale of the mass murder was gradually revealed.

New technology

The final year of the war saw many new weapons, some with the potential to change the course of the war.

By 1943 the Germans had developed a jet fighter, the Me 262, with a top speed of 870 km/h unmatched by any other aircraft. By the time the plane was actually used in combat,

however, the numbers were too small to have any significant impact.

The German V-1 and V-2 rockets ('V' for *Vergeltungswaffe*, 'revenge weapon') continued the Blitz on London. The V-1 could be shot down by fighter planes, but the V-2, powered by a rocket engine, flew much faster and higher and exploded without warning. This missile could be devastating – nearly 600 people died when a single V-2 hit a crowded cinema in Antwerp on 16 December 1944.

The Allies wrought a terrible revenge, most famously through the bombing of Dresden. Over 3,400 tonnes of explosives created a firestorm that set the city ablaze for many days, littering the streets with charred corpses, including many children. Many refugees from eastern Germany were in the city at the time, so the total number killed is hard to estimate. It may have been as high as 135,000 people – more destructive than either of the nuclear bombs dropped on Japan. Was Dresden an important rail hub, as Air Marshal Arthur 'Bomber' Harris argued, or was the attack simply an attempt to punish the Germans?

Weird weapons and tactics

What was the maddest scheme of the war?
You decide:

Britain

- The Rotabuggy, a Jeep with rotors that could be dropped behind enemy lines, was seen as a stepping stone to a Rotatank that could glide down to the ground. The project never really got off the ground.

- The British planned to build a huge, almost unsinkable aircraft carrier out of *pykrete*, a mix of ice and sawdust that was as hard as concrete and took a very long time to melt. Named HMS *Habbakuk* [*sic*], it would be 600 metres long and weigh over 2 million tonnes. The Navy sank the project when it saw the rapidly escalating price tag.

- In 1940 the Directorate of Miscellaneous Weapons Development came up with a plan to build a giant mountain thousands of metres high in Kent, packed with anti-aircraft guns to shoot down the highest-flying German bomber.

- A giant rocket-propelled wheel packed with explosives, known as the Great Panjandrum, was developed to deal with the concrete bunkers along the Normandy coastline. Though the Army spent a fortune testing the device, it was never used in battle.

- British Agents planned to smuggle doses of the female sex hormone oestrogen into Hitler's food to make him less aggressive and more like his gentle younger sister Paula, who worked as a secretary.

- Louis de Wohl, who worked as an astrologer for British intelligence, persuaded them that Hitler was influenced strongly by astrology, and might be likely to choose 'lucky' astrological dates for major operations.

- Other hare-brained British schemes involved dropping poisonous snakes or glue on enemy troops and disguising bombs in tins of fruit imported into Germany.

Germany

- A device known as *der gebone Lauf* ('the curved barrel') was a curved extension to a gun barrel, fitted with a mirror sight, allowing German soldiers to shoot around corners.

- Weighing 180 tonnes, the positively obese Panzerkampfwagen VIII *Maus* tank had a gun big enough to blow any enemy tank apart at middle range. But it was so heavy that no engine could make it trundle along faster than 13 km/h, and it was too heavy to cross most bridges.

- The *Silbervogel* ('silver bird') was a revolutionary design for its time, a sort of early Space Shuttle. In theory, it would be able to cross the Atlantic, drop a 4,000 kg bomb on America, then continue to a landing site in the Pacific, where the Japanese would pick it up and return to sender.

- Nazi scientists also came up with a variety of unusual projectiles. The Vortex Gun fired shells containing coal dust and a slow-burning explosive. In theory, they would create a man-made tornado that would send enemy planes spiralling out of the sky. The so-called Wind Cannon, meanwhile, fired a projectile of compressed air and water vapour, but the test weapon failed to bring down any aircraft. The Sound Cannon created such a loud note that it would kill anyone within 50 metres who heard it for more than a few seconds.

- The Death Ray. In the 1930s, Nazi agents spread the rumour that German scientists were building a Sun Gun, a giant mirror in space that could frazzle an entire city using radio waves. British boffin Robert Watson-Watt was asked if a death ray could work. No, he replied, but radio waves might be used to spot a plane – and so radar was born.

United States

- Psychologist B. F. Skinner devised a plan for pigeon-guided missiles for the US Navy. A camera on the front of the missile recorded its flight path, which was then projected on a screen for the pigeon to see. The birds were trained to recognise the missile's intended target, and they would peck at the screen if it was drifting off course. This information was fed to the weapon's flight controls, which would then be changed to reflect the new co-ordinates.

- US intelligence came up with a number of mid-boggling devices, from Aunt Jemima – an explosive that resembled pancake flour – to 'mule turds', booby-trapped explosives disguised as dung. 'Who? Me?' was a below-the-belt chemical weapon that smelled like dung, crammed into a tube. It was given to children in Chinese cities to humiliate Japanese officers by squirting it on the seat of their pants.

- Project Rainbow, or the Philadelphia Experiment. One conspiracy theory claims that a secret Navy experiment conducted at the Philadelphia Naval Shipyard around 28 October 1943 made an entire ship vanish into thin air. If you believe the story – surely a hoax – the destroyer USS Eldridge became invisible for 15 minutes and was teleported across space and time.

To the bitter end

'We shall not capitulate . . . no, never.
We may be destroyed, but if we are, we shall
drag the world with us . . . a world in flames.'

Hitler decides to go down fighting

In the last months of the war, so many Germans continued to die needlessly, whether civilians slaughtered by the Red Army or by Allied bombing, or the young boys of the Hitler Youth battling Soviet tanks with rifles and grenades. Why did Nazi Germany carry on fighting?

On 20 July 1944 a German colonel, Claus von Stauffenberg, left a bomb in the Führer's office. It exploded, just missing its target, and the following day the rebel officer was shot. Ironically Stauffenberg's brave attempt, the closest anyone came to assassinating Hitler, created a sudden surge in support for the Nazi regime.

'Enjoy the war – the peace will be much worse.'

A joke amongst Berliners in 1945

Fear was also a powerful motivator. Joseph Goebbels, Hitler's propaganda wizard, did his best to persuade Germans that the fight must go on: if they lost the war the next stop was death or a prison camp in Siberia. Meanwhile the Nazi secret police, the Gestapo, snooped on every street corner and arrested, tortured and killed thousands of suspects.

Some Germans carried on simply out of habit: as the Red Army fought its way to Berlin, civil servants struggled through the ruins for a day at the office. The Germans were remarkably efficient at keeping everything going despite the carnage, moving factories underground or replacing workers with slave labour.

In March the Allies crossed their last major hurdle, the Rhine, and began to advance rapidly across Germany. It was a race against the Russians to be the first into Berlin. By February 1945, however, the Red Army was waiting on the river Oder, just outside Berlin, with 2.5 million men and 6,000 tanks. All that stood in their way was a ragged German army filled with old men and young boys, and desperately short of ammunition.

Throughout March and April, Hitler's generals begged him to surrender. The Führer refused to listen. From 1 April he was holed up in a bunker some 15 metres below the streets of Berlin, along with his partner Eva Braun and several high-ranking Nazi ministers, including Hitler's top aide Martin Bormann, and Goebbels. Though Braun had been Hitler's mistress for many years, she had little involvement in politics (or Nazi war crimes), and might well have been treated leniently by the Allies after the war; yet she stayed with Hitler to the end.

By now the Führer had lost the plot, giving orders to non-existent armies and demanding that the entire country die fighting. By 24 April Berlin was ringed by Soviet soldiers. On 28 April Hitler learned that SS leader Heinrich Himmler – the man behind the Nazi death camps – was negotiating a surrender with the Allies.

The game was up. On the afternoon of 30 April, Hitler said goodbye to his staff then shot himself in the head. Eva Braun had swallowed poison a few minutes before. The

bodies were taken outside, cremated with petrol and buried. On the following day, Goebbels and his wife poisoned their six children in the bunker, then asked an SS guard to shoot them. The Third Reich, meant to last a thousand years, was over in twelve.

Germany surrendered unconditionally on 7 May 1945, and the following day was celebrated as VE (Victory in Europe) Day. The were wild celebrations across America. In London, huge crowds outside Buckingham Palace cheered Churchill, George VI and Queen Elizabeth.

VE Day at Buckingham Palace

Where are they now?

Hitler and Nazi survival stories are ten a penny, from far-fetched tales of underground bases in the Canadian Arctic and plastic surgery to more plausible stories of Nazi colonies in South America. Operation Paperclip, however, is no myth. Hoping to plunder Germany's scientific secrets, US intelligence invited hundreds of Nazi scientists and doctors to come to America after the war, especially anyone involved with rockets, nerve gas, jet aircraft or guided missiles. Over the next 20 years over 1,500 scientists accepted the offer, including some with links to slave-labour camps and human experimentation. Yet all of these men were cleared for work in America. It's no coincidence that cruise missiles are still based on the design of the V-1 rocket.

Hitler's ghost haunted the Soviets for years to come. Stalin wanted proof that Hitler was dead, so part of the Führer's charred skull was dug up and shipped to Moscow, where it was hidden away in a box until 1991. Meanwhile the rest of Hitler's skeleton was reburied in a Soviet military base. According to a former KGB general, some 25 years later, in 1970, the fear of a neo-Nazi revival was so great that the Führer's remains were secretly burnt in a night-time operation, then ground into dust and tipped into the sewerage system in Magdeburg, East Germany.

No Surrender!

In the Far East the war continued to rage. The British advanced further in Burma, and on 9 February 1945 the Americans attacked Iwo Jima – the first patch of Japanese land to be invaded in 4,000 years. Retreat was simply not an option for the 20,000 troops who defended this small island. When the island was taken on 16 March, just 216 Japanese soldiers were taken prisoner. The rest fought to the death.

The next stepping stone to Japan was the island of Okinawa. Japanese defenders hidden in a network of caves and tunnels – plus torrential rain – added up to a rerun of First World War-style trench warfare that lasted from 1 April to 22 June. Not for nothing is the battle known in Japan as the 'typhoon of steel': the US forces suffered over 55,000 casualties, while kamikaze attacks sank 32 ships and damaged 368 more. The Japanese lost 100,000 troops, along with tens of thousands of local civilians who were killed, wounded or committed suicide.

The Americans were now just 500 km away from Japan, with the Red Army all set to join in from the north. But the attack on Okinawa proved that any US assault on the Japanese mainland would result in a bloodbath. It was time for the Americans to unleash their secret weapon.

Since the early 1930s, scientists had known that splitting the atom could create an earth-shattering new weapon – the atomic bomb. By 1941 Roosevelt was willing to invest huge sums to ensure that the Americans would win the race to build the first bomb, one of the greatest engineering feats in history. US and British teams joined forces in the Manhattan Project based at Los Alamos in New Mexico, and on 16 July 1945 the first test bomb was exploded in the desert with a force equivalent to 17,000 tonnes of high explosive.

Harry S. Truman, the new US president following Roosevelt's death in April, agreed to use the bomb against a human target. On the morning of 6 August 1945 the B-29 Superfortress *Enola Gay* dropped the bomb *Little Boy* on the Japanese city of Hiroshima,

a military supply base with shipyards, weapons factories – and a population of 300,000. As the dreaded mushroom cloud erupted, two thirds of the city was destroyed in an instant, including 80,000 people. Another 80,000 died from radiation poisoning in the coming months and years.

Three days later another bomb, codenamed *Fat Man*, was dropped on Nagasaki by another B-29. The effects were equally devastating. Incredibly, though the Japanese emperor Hirohito and three of his ministers wanted the fighting to stop, the three other officers in the Supreme War Council refused to surrender. While they deliberated, 700 US bombers dropped a further 4,500 tonnes of explosives on Japan on 14 August.

At noon the next day, Hirohito announced the Japanese surrender, speaking to his people for the first time. Despite this, the Japanese army in Manchuria fought on until 22 August, battling against a powerful invasion force from the Soviet Union, which had declared war on Japan only a fortnight before.

30 years in the jungle

Lieutenant Hiroo Onoda of the Japanese Imperial Army's Intelligence Division was sent to the Philippine Island of Lubang in 1944 with a mission to launch guerrilla attacks from behind the lines. When US planes dropped leaflets over the island in August 1945 telling them the war was over, Onoda and his four-man unit believed it was a trick. For years they continued to carry out raids against local police stations and US patrols, surviving on rice, coconuts and bananas.

By 1972, two of his team had been killed and the other had surrendered. Onoda fought on alone. Two years later a Japanese college student found his hideout deep in the Filipino jungle. On 10 March 1975, 29 years after the start of his mission, Onoda finally came out of the jungle. Wearing his immaculately kept full-dress uniform, he surrendered his sword to Filipino president Ferdinand Marcos. During his time on the island, Onoda and his men had killed over 30 Filipinos and Americans and wounded over 100 more people, but under the circumstances he was pardoned.

The formal Japanese surrender was signed on September 2 on the deck of the USS *Missouri*, anchored in Toyko Bay.

The news of the end of the war, known as VJ (Victory over Japan) Day, led to more festivities in the victorious countries. A giant conga formed along Oxford Street in London while 2 million people thronged New York's Times Square. In Japan, people wept openly in humiliation at their country's defeat.

A world turned upside down

The war was over, six years and a day after it had begun. Germany and Japan had been defeated – but was it worth it?

Unlike the end of World War One, when huge changes were made to the map of Europe, very few borders were redrawn. People were moved instead. Millions of Germans had fled west to escape the wrath of the advancing Soviet forces. Another 11.5 million Germans were expelled from Eastern Europe after the war, including 2.2 million from Czechoslovakia and some 3 million from Poland.

In Germany, 5.5 million Soviet citizens were sent home. Instead of a warm welcome, most were treated like criminals for having been slave workers, and were given long prison sentences. During the war Stalin had also shipped 300,000 German settlers along the Volga River to Siberia. Some people never returned home, including most of the Poles who fought alongside the British. Surviving Jews from concentration camps who returned to their homes often found they were not welcome.

The refugee crisis cast a long shadow – it was 1960 before the United Nations was able to close the final refugee camps in Europe. In other parts of the world, the problem lingered on for decades.

At a conference in February 1945, in the Soviet resort of Yalta, the Allied leaders Churchill, Stalin and Roosevelt had decided to split Germany into four zones policed by the United States, Britain, France and Russia. By the end of the war, however, Churchill had been beaten in an election and Roosevelt was dead.

Grim statistics

World War Two was the most destructive event in history:

- An estimated 70 million people died, and, for the first time in history, more of these were civilians than combatants. The Soviet Union (28 million), China (possibly 15 million or more), Poland (6.8 million), Germany (7 million) and Japan (3.6 million) suffered the most deaths.

- The Nazi genocide killed at least 11 million people, 6 million of them Jews, while Japan's policies resulted in the deaths of 17 million civilians in Asia.

- What Churchill so grimly described as 'the hot rake of war' devastated millions of homes, hospitals, factories, particularly on the Eastern Front, due to the 'scorched earth' policy of both sides. In Russia, over 1,700 towns and 70,000 villages were destroyed. The industrial resources of Poland and France were halved, while Great Britain had lost half of her merchant navy.

Peace and retribution

The new British prime minister, Clement Attlee, met with Stalin and new US president Harry S. Truman at Potsdam in July 1945. They agreed to set up a tribunal at Nuremberg, which sentenced eleven former Nazi leaders to death, while seven Japanese leaders were hanged after a similar trial in Asia. Other war criminals were given long jail sentences. Ordinary Germans were taken to see films of death camps such as Auschwitz, to show them the true nature of the Nazi regime.

Stalin now controlled – through trade agreements, diplomacy and the threat of force – most of the states that the Red Army had liberated from the Nazis. He decided to use these countries as a barrier against a future attack from the West, which became known as the Iron Curtain. By 1948 Albania, Bulgaria, Czechoslovakia, Hungary, Poland, Romania and Yugoslavia all had Communist governments. From a Western point of view, this was a disappointing end to a war that had begun with the intention of liberating Poland from dictatorship.

The Nazi hunters

- Late in 1944 the British army created the Jewish Brigade, made up of Palestinian Jews. One unit fought in Italy, while others helped tens of thousands of concentration-camp survivors to reach Palestine. Some Jewish troops carried out spy or sabotage missions behind German lines.

- When the conflict in Europe ended, some of these Jewish soldiers formed 'revenge squads' and scoured Germany and Austria looking for perpetrators of the Holocaust. They hunted down and killed some 1,500 high-ranking Nazis.

- After the war, individuals such as Simon Wiesenthal and Tuviah Friedman also hunted down former Nazis involved in the Holocaust. Notable targets include Adolf Eichmann, who was smuggled from Argentina by Israeli agents then tried in Israel, and Klaus Barbie, the 'Butcher of Lyon', who was eventually extradited from Bolivia and tried in France.

- Russian officers in 1945 were told to shoot any Nazi official from the rank of mayor up.

- Collaborators in many European countries were also punished. In France, 120,000 received prison sentences and 800 were executed. Another 10,000 were murdered in the years after the war.

Europe was now divided into the democratic countries in Western Europe and the Communist Eastern bloc. Tensions rose in June 1948, when the Soviet Union cut off the West's land access to the American, British and French sectors of Berlin. Britain and the United States responded by airlifting food and supplies into the city until the blockade was called off 11 months later.

Germany was now two countries, East and West Germany, the East being Communist. The division was marked in 1961 by the building of the Berlin Wall. The Wall (which would stand until 1989) became a symbol of the so-called Cold War between two superpowers: the United States and the Soviet Union. For the next 30 years there was a very real fear that the Red Army could sweep through Europe at any moment.

Many of the great powers before the war, such as Britain, France, Germany and Japan, were now seriously weakened. In the years that followed, many of their former colonies achieved independence.

The real winners?

Some did very well out of the war:

- Huge profits were made by selling rationed goods like cigarettes, chocolate, coffee and butter on the black market. During the Battle of the Bulge in January 1945, 200 US deserters were captured trying to steal an entire trainload of soap, food, cigarettes and other supplies.

- Cigarette manufacturers certainly did well. Cigarettes were included in the C-rations given to GIs, and by the end of the war cigarette sales were at an all-time high. In 1942 the American Tobacco Company changed the Lucky Strike package from green to white with the slogan 'Lucky Strike Green Has Gone to War.' The ad campaign coincided with the US landings in North Africa – and sales increased by 38 per cent.

- Swiss banks traded Nazi gold for Swiss francs, allowing the Nazis to buy machinery from Switzerland, including over 80 per cent of Swiss munitions exports. In 2000 one of the world's biggest banks, UBS of Switzerland, admitted exploiting Nazi slave labourers during World War Two. The bank owned a cement factory where SS officers forced at least 400 prisoners from the nearby Auschwitz concentration camp to work.

- Many German businesses profited from slave labour, including Volkswagen and Siemens. Of the 35,000 slave labourers who worked for I.G. Farben (a pharmaceuticals and chemicals giant) at Auschwitz, over 25,000 died there.

- During the war, US computer giant IBM's punch-card machines were used by the Nazis to help transport the Jews more efficiently to concentration camps such as Auschwitz.

- US car manufacturers General Motors and Ford controlled 70 per cent of the German car market when war broke out in 1939. In the run-up to war, they retooled their factories to supply trucks and aeroplanes to the German army and air force for the Blitzkrieg campaigns.

- There's a story that the fizzy drink Fanta was created for the Nazis by Coca-Cola. The reality is a little more complex. When the war started, the Coca-Cola factory in Germany, cut off from the parent company, was unable to get the ingredients for Coca-Cola. To keep his staff employed, the local boss, Max Keith (who was not a Nazi member), decided to create a completely new drink and asked his sales team to come up with a 'fantastic' name for it. One of them blurted out 'Fanta', and a brand was born. At the end of the war, Keith handed back the factory (and its profits) to the parent company in America.

There was no repeat of the harsh war reparations handed out at the Treaty of Versailles in 1919. The United States was just too worried about the spread of Communism. From 1948, the US Marshall Plan gave around $13 billion in aid to European countries, regardless of which side they had fought on. In Japan, a US army of occupation under General Douglas MacArthur helped to create a stable, democratic government. Within 35 years, Japan had one of the world's most successful economies, while the Marshall Plan paved the way for the European Union.

The impact of the war is still felt in many other parts of the world. After the Holocaust, many Jews fled to Palestine, then under British control. When the British left in 1948, they created the new state of Israel – resented to this day by surrounding Arab nations.

If all this seems a terrible price to pay for victory, imagine what the world might have been like today had Nazism triumphed. We owe a great debt to millions of ordinary men and women who were willing to sacrifice everything for what they believed in.

Glossary

Allies The nations that fought against the Axis forces: chiefly France, Great Britain and its Empire, the Soviet Union and the United States of America.

Anschluss The Nazi occupation of Austria in 1938.

Aryan The Nazi term for 'pure-blooded' Germans.

Axis The alliance between Germany, Italy and Japan during World War Two, joined by other nations such as Romania, Hungary, Croatia and Bulgaria.

blitzkrieg A 'lightning attack' using planes, tanks and armoured vehicles to punch a hole in the enemy line.

blockade The use of ships to prevent supplies getting through to enemy ports.

commando A special forces soldier used to make sudden, destructive raids against enemy targets.

concentration camp A prison camp where civilians and others are kept under armed guard.

conscription Forcing citizens to join the army by law.

convoy A group of merchant ships sailing together, escorted by warships to protect against submarines.

counter-attack An attack by a defending force.

D-Day The day on which an operation is due to begin – especially the Normandy landings of 6 June 1944.

death camp A concentration camp where the inmates are murdered or forced to work to death.

Eastern Front The battle lines between Germany and the Soviet Union.

evacuate To send people or goods to a place of safety.

Final Solution A euphemism for the Nazi plan to exterminate all Jews.

flak Anti-aircraft fire.

Gestapo The secret police of Nazi Germany.

GI An American soldier.

Holocaust The systematic murder of millions of Jews and other peoples by the Nazis in World War Two.

Home Front Life for civilians during the war.

incendiary bomb A bomb designed to cause fires.

KGB The Soviet secret police.

Luftwaffe The German air force.

MI5 The British military intelligence service.

neutral Not supporting either side in a war.

occupied Europe The parts of Europe conquered and ruled by Germany during World War Two.

offensive An attack or series of attacks.

paramilitary Organised like an army.

partisan A resistance fighter.

propaganda Books, films and other media that spread ideas, rumours or lies, often to help one side in a war.

radar A device that uses radio waves to track enemy ships and aircraft.

RAF The British Royal Air Force.

Red Army The army of the Soviet Union.

reparations Compensation payments.

resistance Secret organisations that worked to overthrow German rule in occupied Europe.

sabotage Destroying property to hinder an enemy, often behind enemy lines.

SS An elite Nazi army unit that also operated as Hitler's bodyguard and as a special security force. *SS* stands for *Schutzstaffel*, German for 'protection squad'.

U-boat A German submarine (from the German *Unterseeboot*, 'undersea boat').

Wehrmacht The German army.

Timeline of World War Two

1939

23 August Nazis and Soviets sign Pact of Steel.

1 September Germany invades Poland. War begins.

3 September Britain and France declare war on Germany.

30 November Soviet Union attacks Finland.

1940

9 April German forces invade Norway and Denmark.

10 May Germany invades Belgium, Luxembourg, the Netherlands and France.

27 May Evacuation of British forces at Dunkirk.

10 June Italy enters World War Two.

22 June France surrenders to Germany.

10 July Battle of Britain air campaign begins.

7 September German Blitz against Britain begins.

1941

11 March US President Roosevelt signs Lend-Lease Act.

6 April Germany invades Yugoslavia and Greece.

22 June Germans and their allies invade Soviet Union.

31 July Nazis begin systematic mass murder of Jews.

6 December Soviet counter-attack drives German forces back and saves Moscow.

7 December Japan bombs US Navy base at Pearl Harbor.

8 December United States declares war on Japan.

11 December Germany and Italy declare war on US.

1942

2–12 January Japanese forces advance rapidly in Asia, invading Philippines, Indonesia, Malaysia and Burma.

January Mass murder by gassing begins at Auschwitz.

15 February Singapore surrenders to Japanese forces.
30 May First 1,000-bomber raid on Germany.
4 June US Navy halts Japanese advance at Midway.
23–24 October British troops defeat German and
Italian forces at El Alamein in Egypt.

1943

2 February German 6th Army surrenders to the Soviets
at Stalingrad, the first major defeat for Hitler.
8 February US forces capture Guadalcanal from Japan.
16–20 March Battle of Atlantic peaks with 27 merchant
ships sunk by German U-boats.
16 May Germans crush Jewish uprising in Warsaw.
5 July Germans mount offensive against Soviets at Kursk.
10 July Allied invasion of Sicily.
8 September Italy surrenders. Germans occupy Italy.

1944

6 January Soviet troops advance into Poland.
6 June D-Day: Allied forces invade Normandy, France.
25 August Paris liberated by Allied forces.
20 October Battle of Leyte Gulf, major victory for US
Navy over Japanese. US troops land in Philippines.
16–27 December Battle of the Bulge, final German attack.

1945

27 January Soviet troops liberate Auschwitz.
26 March US Marines capture island of Iwo Jima.
16 April Soviet forces surround Berlin.
30 April Adolf Hitler commits suicide in Berlin bunker.
7 May Germany surrenders. End of war in Europe.
21 June US Marines capture island of Okinawa.
6 August Hiroshima destroyed by US atomic bomb.
14 August Japan surrenders and war finally ends.

Index

INDEX